Are You Ready to Restructure?

To Robyn, Laurel, and Genevieve,
with the hope that your education
will be just a bit better as a result.

Are You Ready to Restructure?

A Guidebook for
Educators, Parents, and
Community Members

David T. Conley

CORWIN PRESS, INC.
A Sage Publications Company
Thousand Oaks, California

Copyright © 1996 by Corwin Press, Inc.

For information address:

Corwin Press, Inc.
A Sage Publications Company
2455 Teller Road
Thousand Oaks, California 91320
E-mail: order@corwin.sagepub.com

SAGE Publications Ltd.
6 Bonhill Street
London EC2A 4PU
United Kingdom

SAGE Publications India Pvt. Ltd.
M-32 Market
Greater Kailash I
New Delhi 110 048 India

Printed in the United States of America

Library of Congress Cataloging-in-Publication Data

Conley, David T., 1948-
    Are you ready to restructure? A guidebook for educators,
parents, and community members / David T. Conley.
        p. cm.
    Includes bibliographical references.
    ISBN 0-8039-6194-4 (C : alk. paper).—ISBN 0-8039-6195-2 (P :
alk. paper)
    1. Educational change—United States. 2. School management and
organization—United States. 3. Education—United States—Aims and
objectives. I. Title.
LB2805.C615   1995
371.2'00973—dc20   95-40434

This book is printed on acid-free paper.

96 97 98 99 10 9 8 7 6 5 4 3 2 1

Production Editor: Diana E. Axelsen   Typesetter: Christina M. Hill

Contents

PART II
What Does Restructuring Look Like?

PART III
How Will Roles Change for Educators and Community Members?

PART IV
How Can a School Begin to Restructure?

About the Author

David T. Conley is Associate Professor of Educational Policy and Management in the College of Education at the University of Oregon. He teaches courses on school restructuring, educational policy, school improvement, educational leadership, teacher leadership, and supervision and evaluation. He has conducted studies of schools involved in restructuring and served as a consultant for schools and districts pursuing fundamental change, and as education policy consultant for the Oregon Business Council. He frequently gives presentations locally, nationally, and internationally on restructuring and has published extensively on the topic.

He contributed to the development and implementation of Oregon's 1991 school restructuring bill, the Oregon Education Act for the 21st Century. He recently facilitated a 2-year U.S. Department of Education grant designed to enable nine schools to take "the next step" in restructuring.

Dr. Conley is currently on assignment to the Oregon State System of Higher Education as the director of the Proficiency-based Admission Standards System (PASS) Project. This project is to design and implement the nation's first college admission system based on student performance, not Carnegie units. He has written and received over $3.2 million in grants from public and private agencies to support this effort. He can be reached at the PASS Project. P.O. Box 3175, Eugene, OR, 97403-0175 or by telephone at (541) 346-5799.

Before joining the faculty at the University of Oregon, he spent 18 years serving as a school administrator and teacher in Colorado and California. He received his Ph.D. in educational administration and his

M.A. in social foundations of education from the University of Colorado, Boulder, and his B.A. in social sciences from the University of California, Berkeley.

Introduction

This book is designed to be a resource for people who want to give serious thought to changing their schools in some fundamental fashion. To achieve this aim, it includes material of interest not only to administrators, teachers, and boards of education, but also to parents, community members, and many students.

Leaders in both the private and public sectors realize that those who do frontline work need to be involved in making decisions about how their organization is run, and they also need to be capable of making good decisions. They need both information and opportunity. This book will help provide people in schools, education's front line, with better information to use as they make decisions that will affect their schools.

When participation in schools is expanded, everyone needs greater access to information related to normal operations and functions of the school or district. However, very different kinds of information are needed when a school considers whether it should engage in changes that affect its basic functioning and organization.

It is often difficult to gain access to information of any sort to help in making such far-reaching decisions. People who do not have access to information are very unlikely to do much beyond maintaining current procedures. Many schools have instituted governance groups, often called site councils. They are relatively new, and their work is often scrutinized closely. Site-based governing groups without information about the current state of the school, the rationale for change, and an outline of what is possible will have difficulty improving their school or offering guidance on more fundamental change. They will tend to reinvent the present system. The same maxim applies to administrators and boards of education, as well.

I offer in this volume an informational resource guide that presents in plain, straightforward language a summary of the current issues in school restructuring. I draw extensively from work published earlier in a larger and more detailed book titled *Roadmap to Restructuring*. That publication, approximately 400 pages in length, drew from more than 600 different sources to illustrate the range of restructuring ideas and activities. In it, I quoted extensively from those sources to provide the reader with a detailed picture of the thinking that has shaped the educational restructuring movement during the 1990s.

This book draws from and builds upon many of the conclusions reached in *Roadmap to Restructuring*. I attempt here to be brief in order to offer the reader more ideas and information in fewer pages. I am aware of how difficult it is for busy educators, parents, community members, and students to find time to read educational treatises. At the same time, it's vitally important that people who are involved in educational restructuring have the broadest perspective possible. I seek to provide viewpoints on the need and rationale for change along with specific techniques and strategies that schools use to restructure.

One of the most valuable things that can occur when people with many differing perspectives and backgrounds become involved in the change process is a sharing, exchanging, and debating of ideas. Rather than rubber-stamping someone else's agenda, or adopting someone else's program, a vigorous exchange of ideas helps define what is best and what is right for the school. Task forces, study groups, site councils, even faculty meetings can become environments where new approaches and strategies are examined, debated, adapted, and, finally, adopted.

This book serves as a resource to help people engage in a healthy, informed discussion of restructuring possibilities. Each chapter is similar in structure and designed to stand on its own. Each is short enough to be quickly read and then discussed at regular meetings of a group investigating restructuring at a school. To facilitate such discussions, each chapter concludes with a series of questions that raises key issues designed to focus the group's attention and deliberations. These questions are the springboard for more in-depth, possibly more revealing, conversations about the way the school functions currently and the amount of change that will be necessary, possible, or desirable.

This book can be used in a variety of ways to facilitate decision making. Different individuals can be given the responsibility to read and summarize the key points in each chapter and identify their implications for the school; or a group may choose to focus on one chapter and have all members read and discuss that chapter. Similarly, a team might analyze a chapter, refer back to *Roadmap to Restructuring* to identify the key source material related to that chapter, and then find and reproduce those articles or documents for the faculty or the group. Or individuals can be assigned source articles to read and abstract. These abstracts are then copied and assembled in notebook form to allow others easier, quicker access to ideas on the topic being discussed.

All of these techniques are intended to provide information in a concise form to those charged with making decisions about the function and future of the school. In this book, I suggest many other techniques, including visiting other school sites, attending conferences, hearing from experts, and participating in training activities. All of these should be used when appropriate. This book can serve as a starting point: By reading and discussing it, all members of the group will have a common starting point and vocabulary to use when talking about educational change and restructuring. This is particularly valuable for groups that include noneducators as well as educators.

I also include several resources. They suggest the next steps that a group can take in its studies of restructuring. The resources include listings of organizations and key sources in the area of restructuring.

If this book is successful, it will spark creativity, suggest possibilities, generate debate (and disagreement), and, in general, stimulate a group to think about the complexity and content of educational restructuring at the school level. All of this will be only the first step in a long and challenging journey of educational redesign. But even a long journey begins with a single step.

Are You Ready to Restructure?

As the title of the book implies, you need to ask yourself one fundamental question: Are you ready to restructure? "Ready" has two meanings. First, are you psychologically ready to entertain the idea that it is time for fundamental change, not in schooling in the abstract, not in some distant school, not at the state level, but in the way education occurs at your school? Are you ready to entertain the notion that it may be time to examine many deeply held beliefs and assumptions and, possibly, to alter them? Opening oneself to this type of deep introspection is difficult and disturbing. Most people avoid it for as long as possible. Being "ready" to restructure means being prepared to look within the structure of the school and within one's personal belief system to determine the degree to which each benefits students and the degree to which each may be hindering student success.

The other meaning of "ready" is that, having accepted the need to change rather fundamentally, are you equipped to do so? Do you have agreement on basic terms, basic goals, and overall strategies and approaches? Or do people think about the problem so differently, use such different vocabulary to describe similar phenomena, and have such divergent views on the current state of affairs that it is impossible to begin true communication?

A good place to begin to work toward common understanding is by offering a definition of restructuring. By so doing, the group will need to see if there is agreement about the basic nature of the phenomenon. Can people agree on what it means to restructure? Are people willing to consider the implications of agreeing that there is a need to do so? To stimulate such discussion, I contrast three different levels of change—renewal, reform, and restructuring—and then offer a definition of the term *restructuring*.

In education, the term *restructuring* is as notable for its ambiguity as for its meaning. In the private sector, the term has come to mean a process of rapid adaptation prompted by the need to maintain or regain competitiveness. Employment and work assignment patterns within a company are usually disrupted by this process, and layoffs frequently occur as a result. This is not the meaning for this term as educators apply it to change in schools. In fact, educators often do not distinguish very carefully among renewal, reform, and restructuring.

Renewal activities are those that help the organization to do better and/or more efficiently what it is already doing. Most school improvement projects fall into this category, as do many of the staff development programs that districts offer. It is very easy for faculties to assume that if they are undertaking a number of important renewal activities, they are "restructuring," because these activities take a great deal of energy and are capable of yielding positive results. This type of program, however, does not cause schools to examine any of their fundamental assumptions or practices, except by implication. For many schools, renewal may be the most appropriate way to proceed. For others, renewal efforts cloaked as restructuring will lead to frustration and will not achieve the goals for which they were initially intended.

Reform-driven activities are those that alter existing procedures, rules, and requirements to enable the organization to adapt the way it functions to new circumstances or requirements. Two important points help to identify and define reform-oriented efforts: First, changes center on procedural elements, which are the policies and procedures that determine the basic "rules of the game" for all participants in the system; and, second, the impetus for reform almost always comes from some external force, such as a board of education, a state department of education, or even educational reformers. This impetus results in the appointment of committees to examine current practice and to bring the school into conformity with the new expectations or requirements.

Clearly, reform-oriented change cannot be overlooked. At the same time, such activities are more likely to produce a new set of rules or procedures than to result in an examination of fundamental practices or assumptions about schooling. Many externally originated programs of change fail at least in part because teachers do not develop ownership of the program nor do they adapt it to their needs. As in the case of renewal activities, schools can devote a great deal of energy to reform-based improvements and never realize that they have not engaged in a consideration of issues related to restructuring.

If renewal and reform are inadequate to meet the need for change in today's schools, how is restructuring different? The following definition highlights the differences.

Restructuring activities change fundamental assumptions, practices, and relationships, both within the organization and between the organization and the outside world, in ways that lead to improved and varied student learning outcomes for essentially all students. In restructuring, fundamental assumptions must be challenged for change to occur. Furthermore, student learning must be the focus of all activities. When we say that learning is to be improved and varied, it implies not just brief memorization of factual material, but the ability to retain, synthesize, and apply complex information in meaningful ways, particularly as such application demonstrates understanding of challenging content. The definition highlights the need to examine learning through a variety of lenses and to examine all current assumptions, practices, and relationships in light of a single, overarching goal: enhancing students' learning. It also draws attention to the needs of all students attending school, not just those students who are currently succeeding.

Many educators seem to view restructuring as a way to create the appearance of change without necessarily confronting the harsh realities that fundamental changes suggest. These educators seem to say: "I'm all for change—as long as I don't have to do anything differently." Or they say, "Restructuring? Yes, I think we did that last year." This unwillingness to look at underlying assumptions, values, beliefs, practices, and relationships can prevent schools from coming to grips with the profound and disturbing implications of many current practices and of true restructuring.

It seems likely that any district or school that adopts the definition of restructuring presented previously would find itself examining almost all its practices. For most schools, such self-examination is too difficult and threatening. Schools should not feel so alone in this respect. In the corporate world, companies rarely take a close look at all their practices in the absence of some external challenge or threat and an ensuing internal crisis. Any organization, including a school, should strive to change before it is threatened by a crisis. Those individuals with responsibilities for governing schools should ask themselves whether it is time to examine their basic assumptions, beliefs, and practices, and whether failure to do so will result in a crisis for the school in the foreseeable future.

DISCUSSION QUESTIONS

1. What is our definition of *restructuring?*
2. What examples of renewal, reform, and restructuring are present in our school?
3. How might this book serve as a resource to help determine if we are ready to restructure?
4. Are there any examples of other organizations in our community that have had to adapt to large-scale change recently? How well have they done? How did they prepare?

PART I

Why Restructure?

1 *Perspectives on Change in Education*

It's pretty clear that the future is going to be unlike the past in many important ways. It's also pretty clear that our experiences in schools and perceptions of education will likely define how we structure schooling for today's students. There's a problem here. Our current frame of reference for education is almost certainly based on personal experiences in the educational system to a significant degree. This frame of reference is by definition inadequate as a basis for designing the schooling that today's and tomorrow's young people will need to succeed in their lives. And yet it's all we know. How can we resolve this seeming conundrum?

One possible way is to examine all of our current beliefs, assumptions, and educational practices from a fresh perspective. This does not mean that we abandon everything that schools do currently. In fact, many teaching and learning practices are well-established and likely should be continued in any new model of schooling. However, it's very difficult to consider the demands for the future if we limit ourselves to the models of the present as our only options.

Those who propose to change schooling must begin by examining current assumptions and considering a variety of new models. There probably is not any one model of education or right way to redesign schooling for the future. Instead, there are multiple right ways to organize schooling, and the challenge is for people in each community to determine which ways are best for them and their children.

This is a challenging goal. Most schools have not been designed to change, let alone change rapidly. Most teachers, administrators, and parents have neither the extensive experience nor high motivation needed to engage in large-scale educational redesign. However, many schools have adopted systematic school improvement activities during the past 15 to 20 years, and these experiences help adults in those schools be more capable of considering large-scale change. Some schools have never engaged in organized programs of improvement. Administrators, teachers, and parents at these sites have an even greater challenge when asked to suggest new educational structures and programs.

One of the key defining features of restructuring is that people at schools and those affected by schooling are being called upon to lead the redesign process. Decision making has been decentralized; it has been given to schools to make decisions that until recently were made by central offices or state departments of education. This approach assumes that educators and community members will eagerly take this new authority and quickly create efficient, imaginative, high-performing learning environments where the needs of all students are met. This is perhaps expecting too much from people who have had little or no authority or training to achieve these goals.

In some ways, the current strategy of school reform expects educators to act like physicians—highly trained professionals who employ a scientific knowledge base to make major decisions regarding their clients in a personalized environment where the needs of each client can be relatively clearly defined, and where the success of the treatment can be accurately gauged. In fact, educators have been treated more like bureaucrats, who are expected to make few decisions and to demonstrate little initiative. They are to interpret rules and regulations that are promulgated "on high."

What must be done for decentralization and involvement to succeed? First, we must not spend any more time and energy criticizing the people in the current system. The issue here is not that anyone has done anything wrong. Teachers have done exactly what they have been instructed or required to do. So have principals, school boards, and departments of education. Hard-working, dedicated professionals have worked diligently within the constraints of a system, whereas clients' needs have changed dramatically.

Schools have not been able to keep pace with these changing needs, but this is not unusual. Most large organizations in this country (and elsewhere) have had to confront similar challenges. American corporations have gone through a 20-year period of shock and adaptation mostly because of the fact that they had not been adapting gradually to changes in the world around them. The difficulties that corporations have faced as they attempt to reinvent themselves are well-documented. It is little wonder that schools have not adapted any more rapidly than they have when companies that should be able to adapt have not been able to do so. Teachers should not be blamed for the current mismatch that exists between many of their practices and the needs of their students and of society.

Many dedicated teachers have worked, and continue to work, valiantly in a system that in many ways no longer works. Because few teachers see themselves as capable of changing "the system," they do their best to make it work regardless of how difficult or nonsensical the tasks and conditions they are given. Almost all teachers recognize that today's students are different in many ways from those of 20 to 30 years ago, and surveys indicate that many teachers believe it is time for fundamental change in education.

There is less agreement about the specific ways in which schools should change. Many educators believe that students must first come to school ready to learn, with a proper attitude and adequate support from home. Others believe more discipline, or a return to the basics, is the answer. If only students could once again be the way they were, everything would be all right.

Others believe that schools can be changed a little at a time, that by gradually improving this or that aspect of education, schools will be transformed eventually into new, more effective places, and that somehow this change will be achieved without disruption and conflict. In this model of gradual change, teachers, parents, and students will scarcely notice the difference, but in the end will have a much-improved process for schooling.

A third view assumes that change can be achieved only through a reexamination and rethinking of schooling on a more fundamental level. This type of change results in major organizational upheaval and significant amounts of conflict. These changes do not occur unnoticed, or without the involvement and awareness of teachers, students, parents, and community members. Knowing which of these three belief systems about change will guide your school's change process is an important early dimension of readiness.

Throughout the nation, we are sending mixed signals to educators. On one hand, educators are being told to improve dramatically to meet the needs of a changing student population. On the other hand, they are often confronted by harsh criticism if they attempt to change relatively quickly and decisively. Educators also have few new resources to assist them in achieving the goal of higher student achievement. These mixed messages create nearly unmanageable internal tensions for educators considering change, who are faced with many difficult questions. How can they even consider change in light of the current fiscal situation? How can they be suggesting changes that are not tried and proven already? How much change can the school system take at one time? Should they wait until the situation returns to "normal"?

Educational change is going to be difficult. However, difficulties can be softened if educators and community members begin by agreeing upon three things: first, the need and rationale for change; second, the general direction, or vision, that will guide their journey; and third, the overall process to be followed. This is simple enough to say, but each of the three points is very difficult to accomplish.

Many schools have tended to overlook one or two of these points as they approach restructuring. For example, they may agree upon a change process without having achieved agreement on the need for change. They might select a method or process for change without having some sense of the direction in which they are headed. Or they may choose a specific project or program without tying it to a broader vision. Inattention to the complex nature of change generally leads to failure and frustration.

This book is designed to help the reader consider each of these three crucial dimensions: the rationale, content, and process of large-scale change in schooling.

The Role of Research in Restructuring

There are three key phases to the change process. First is creating readiness; second is selecting the things to change; third is implementing the desired changes. This book concentrates on the first, explains many of the options for the second, and considers the issues associated with the third. As important as readiness is, student learning will not improve if schools don't select methods that are effective. Making a decision about what needs to change may be relatively easy; deciding what to do that is better may not be.

Educators have not tended to use research to make changes. They often consider many other factors like expense, convenience, match with local beliefs and conceptions, personal experiences, acceptability to teaching staff, amount of training or retraining required, and so on. The proven effectiveness of a new idea or program is often an afterthought.

The restructuring process offers a golden opportunity to pay more attention to what has been proven to work to improve student learning. Many different educational approaches have been studied extensively during the past 25 years, a period when serious educational research was attempted in earnest. For some educational methods, numerous studies have been conducted. Educators should be ready to examine proven methods and find ways to adopt those that make sense for their schools.

At the same time, educational research is not the same as medical research. Learning is not a disease. Education is not the process of repairing a deficit in the learner in the way that medical care is the treatment of a disease or pathology in an individual. Medical research has been effective because it has been able to focus on specific ailments and devise treatments for them. Successful treatment means curing the particular ailment.

The problem in education is that learning is many things operating in combination. Although learners develop and master distinct skills, what they learn in one area may or may not carry over to another, and if it doesn't, it has to be retaught. As a result, most educational "treatments" are not terribly strong in the way that a medical treatment is or can be. Educational treatments occur in unbounded social environments; they are not limited to the bounded complexity of a human body. The very effective actions of educators can be counteracted by other forces over which educators have no control. The learner can combine learnings in ways that the teacher could never anticipate. Learners are often poor "patients"; they don't follow the "doctor's" advice very well.

The net result is that few educational techniques, however well-documented as successful, will ever show much of an effect all by themselves. Educators and community members who look to educational research for answers can be assured that they will find answers; but they must also keep in mind that these answers are not miracles. Any method, no matter how well-proven, will have to be put into practice within a school that has a history and culture, assumptions and beliefs, social interaction patterns and existing practices, all of which will dilute the effects of any particular method or structure.

In practice, this means that any one change, such as a new schedule, student learning standards, complex assessments, a new teaching technique such as cooperative learning, or a program like a school-within-a-school, is not likely to have a dramatic effect. Some changes may work if the method is uniquely suited to the situation. In general, however, effects will be more subtle. Schools should seek to change things in combination so that the changes reinforce one another. The effect will then be more noticeable.

One of the problems with educational innovation is that educators are often less interested in effects than in implementation. Many programs are adopted, put into place, and not evaluated, . As educators look to restructure, they should be thinking about both the innovations they seek to adopt and how they will track the effects of these innovations once they are adopted.

This advice is particularly applicable to those innovations for which little evidence exists currently on their effectiveness. I do not believe that the only changes a school should undertake are those that have been thoroughly researched and proven effective beyond a doubt. I believe there is a great deal yet to be discovered about how students learn, and many new approaches incorporate techniques already proven effective in other settings. Educators and community members should be free to exercise judgment when approving new programs. Given that few programs have that powerful of an effect on individual learners, and that few decisions have been based on research to begin with, educators have some greater margin for error than do physicians.

What educators are deciding is more akin to developing a well-educated person than to curing a disease. By analogy, this is closer to learning to lead a healthy life than to curing a disease. Leading a healthy life requires many decisions, all having different effects. It requires habits developed over time, and a commitment to maintain behaviors through internal motivation. The research on how to be healthy comes from many sources. Medical research is only one source; psychology, physiology, and nutrition also yield important findings. And, as with educational research, no one recommendation is likely to have a dramatic effect on, say, longevity or quality of life for all people. However, a number of changes made in careful combination and with consideration of the individual's genetics, lifestyle, goals, and motivation can have a very pronounced effect.

To help you make more informed decisions about restructuring, I have included an extended bibliography with sources of information on topics related to restructuring. You will want to go beyond this book to examine these sources. They contain information about effective programs and about organizations engaged in restructuring.

DISCUSSION QUESTIONS

1. In what ways have our own personal beliefs and perspectives been challenged or changed in the past year? Five years? Ten years?

2. In what ways is our school well-suited to change and adapt? In what ways is it not? What unique challenges does it face as it considers restructuring?

3. What has the role of research been in the decisions that have been made about current educational programs and practices? Which are supported by research? Which are not?

4. In what ways does the current system support the efforts of teachers at the school? In what ways does it hinder their efforts?

5. What message is the local community sending about the need to change the school?

6. How do we want to use research and information on current best practices as we consider restructuring?

2 *Rationale for Restructuring*

Many people involved in restructuring have heard skeptics utter phrases such as "I know I've been in teaching a long time when I see the same ideas coming around again," or "Here we go again," or "The more things change, the more they stay the same." These sayings reflect the notion that if educators try a particular innovation once, they should either incorporate it into educational practice for all time or abandon it categorically. In reality, educational innovations come and go, not necessarily or solely because of their effectiveness, but at least in part because of the match between the innovation and society's view of education. As those views change, today's successful educational idea may become tomorrow's failure, and vice versa.

Contrary to the view of many skeptics, public education does change in major ways. Although change may be difficult to detect on a year-to-year basis, the educational system has been evolving since the arrival of the Pilgrims. What may be more difficult to see are the fundamental changes that have occurred over relatively short periods of time. It has happened during the period from the early 1890s through about 1920, when changes of virtually unimaginable proportions washed over the system with regularity. These changes shaped the current system and include "innovations" such as principals and superintendents, large high schools with class periods of standard length, vocational education, modern foreign languages, standardized testing, the Carnegie unit as a measure of learning, the junior high school, social services in the schools, and the nonpartisan volunteer school board.

The notion that an education should prepare youth for the labor force also gained respectability and credence. High schools were to be *comprehensive* institutions; they would educate *all* the youth, though in different ways and toward different ends. Previously, public education had been viewed primarily as a way to enable students to read the Bible, as a place to develop citizens who understood what a democratic society was, and as a vehicle for the transmission of local community values. A grade school education was generally sufficient to serve these purposes.

We are looking at change on a similar level in the 1990s. Many of the ideas being proposed are not brand new. Some were attempted in the late 1960s and early 1970s. Innovations such as flexible scheduling, team teaching, integrated curricula, individualized education, and schools-within-schools were tried then.

There is at least one major difference in the way these innovations might affect schools now versus then. In the 1960s, American society was in social flux. Many of the people who entered teaching at that time believed that schools could be vehicles for social change. The average age of faculties was much younger then, as school officials engaged in several years of frantic hiring to keep pace with the arrival of the baby boom in schools. This younger, perhaps more idealistic, teaching staff tended to make more of a connection between education and social justice. There was a belief that schools could promote the ideals of democratic participation and individual self-worth that the civil rights movement and the "counterculture" represented. These were times when freedom was emphasized and accountability downplayed.

The business community (and many parents) never truly supported or even understood many of the changes that were occurring in schools. By the late 1970s, a more general repudiation of the idealism of the 1960s helped contribute to a swing of the pendulum in the other direction as the "back to basics" movement emerged.

How do the events of the past help us understand the forces that favor fundamental change in education today? There appear to be two distinctly different groups that, for very different reasons, are advocating radical transformation of public education. On one hand, educational reformers promote changes that emphasize active engagement in learning by students, new ways of judging student learning that go beyond standardized tests, allocation of time based on the needs of the learner rather than on the needs of the school schedule, and changes in the student-teacher relationship so that teachers help all students achieve success and meet required standards.

At the same time, the business community has emerged as a strong voice for educational change. Many businesses need a new type of worker as they abandon the traditional factory model in the face of a rapidly evolving world economy. Clearly, the American economic system must adapt quickly to its changing role in the international economic system, from Goliath to partner. The United States will never again dominate the world economy as it did in the period immediately following World War II. American business is defining its niche in the international economy through numerous changes. This niche requires highly skilled workers. Business is viewing education as vital to its success.

The emphasis in the call for school restructuring is not lofty social goals; it is economic and social survival. The emphasis is not on freedom for students, but on accountability for learning. Restructuring represents a reordering of society's priorities for education. Because many educators are not enthusiastic about this reordering of priorities, the most powerful forces for change in education will likely come from outside the ranks of professional educators.

Not everyone agrees that schools need to be restructured. Many teachers and parents, in particular, believe that schools are about as good as can reasonably be expected, and that there is little to be gained by attempting large-scale change in education. At the same time, the world surrounding schools continues to change in many ways. Social, political, and economic systems are evolving (and in some cases imploding) at an ever-increasing rate. Old institutions, beliefs, assumptions, and behaviors no longer seem adequate to explain and cope with the problems and issues that present themselves to citizens in complex societies. Technological breakthroughs also create an ever-changing set of opportunities as well as new skills needed to prosper or to survive.

The Changing Face
of the American Economy

The economic system is transforming in ways that have implications for all social institutions, including schools. Some of the elements of the transformation that have the greatest potential impact upon the schools include the following:

- The transition from a workforce composed predominantly of low-skilled workers and a small, highly educated managerial elite who made decisions to a highly skilled workforce in which frontline workers are key decision makers.

- Increased, unrelenting economic competition from Asia and Europe that has led to an accelerated rate of change in the business world and the necessity for teamwork in the workplace.

- Less access to "guaranteed" jobs for high school dropouts through the old means such as trade unions, one major employer in a community, or use of the "old boy" network; more racial/ethnic/gender diversity in the workplace and concomitant equal employment provisions for hiring that make what one knows more important than who one knows.

- A global economy in which companies function throughout the world, workers may have to travel or live outside the United States to progress in the company, and almost every business needs to understand its relationship to foreign competitors.

- A federal deficit that exploded during the 1980s and continues to occupy much of the federal government's attention in the 1990s, guaranteeing that there will be few additional federal monies available to support education or any other social programs.

- Pressure for no tax increases at both state and federal levels combined with decreased rates of personal income growth that make any increase in governmental revenues unlikely.

- A stable to shrinking workforce that will be composed increasingly of women, minorities, and immigrants, groups traditionally not served well by public education, combined with the expectation that all new entrants into the workforce be educated to some relatively high level of functioning.

- The elimination of middle-management positions throughout the economy during the late 1980s and into the 1990s, which results in responsibility for decision-making being pushed downward, requiring workers who are more able to think and managers who are more able to adapt.

The Changing Face
of American Society

Some of the important social forces operating to produce change that will have an impact on public schools include the following:

- The changing structure of the family in the era of the "postnuclear family," the increase in single-parent families, the concomitant disintegration of extended support networks for families.
- The tendency for any crisis to throw low-income families off balance for an extended period unless some sort of external assistance is available because traditional support networks no longer exist.
- The increase in the number of children who are living in poverty.
- The apparent failure of social welfare and social service programs nationally to address the escalating needs of families.
- A lack of interagency cooperation, which results in duplication and overlap among social service programs and many programs offered by schools.
- The failure of schools as vehicles for desegregation or for equal educational performance for minority students; the increasing polarization along economic and racial lines, particularly in urban areas.
- A decreasing sense of civic responsibility, of social tolerance, of a social contract among citizens for the benefit of all; a lack of understanding of the principles of democratic rule by majority with respect for the rights of the minority; decreasing participation in the electoral process and in decision making at the local level.
- An increase in youth violence and gang activity that signals increasing alienation and isolation among young people.
- An increasingly diverse student population whose culture, background, and values may not be the same as the school's predominant values.
- School systems in which "minorities" are the majority, and there is little acknowledgment of this transformation; in such environments, the term "minority" ceases to have any real meaning, yet continues to be used to identify these groups.

Technological Forces

Technological forces include a broad array of new techniques for organizing, communicating, and disseminating information that raises some of the following issues:

- Knowledge is becoming more accessible to more of the population. Teachers and libraries are not the primary storehouses of society's knowledge. Information need no longer be stored in memory for it to be useful, and the ability to access information is as or more important than the ability to memorize.

- Schools are neither organized nor funded in a way that enables them to keep up with changes in knowledge or changes in technology.

- Textbooks are an obsolete technology, yet they continue to be the primary way in which schools transmit information.

- The structure of knowledge is rapidly evolving. The lines among academic disciplines are no longer very clear, yet schools cling to them as the only way to organize the curriculum.

- Information is less of an end in itself than it is a means to an end. Curricula that focus on information as an end in itself (fact-based rote learning) can be counterproductive by extinguishing the curiosity and inquisitiveness of the learner and providing little practice in problem solving.

- Schools have defined technology as computers only. There are many types of technology in addition to computers that are equally or more important in the information age.

- Schools are not moving to integrate technology, nor are they keeping up with the latest developments; in fact, they are falling further and further behind as the equipment purchased in the 1980s becomes obsolete and is not replaced.

- The Internet in particular and other similar networks provide unparalleled access to information to people within their own homes. The Internet is only in its infancy and is already impressive as a potential learning tool. Schools are not moving systematically to incorporate the Internet into instruction, and, more important, learners do not necessarily need school to access the Internet. Homes are becoming richer in technology, whereas schools are not.

Changing Values Within Society

The observations presented in the previous sections strongly suggest that the world is changing. So are many of the values that shape public discussion of educational goals. In some senses, these shifts are more difficult to perceive than larger social and economic changes. They are often observed only in hindsight. As one looks back over a decade or more, these shifts become more apparent; in day-to-day life, they may be less apparent.

Although many changes in values are occurring, there are six areas in particular that have implications for schooling: (a) the increased value placed on the individual and individual rights, (b) the triumph of the marketplace as an economic model that influences all sectors of society, (c) the rise of democratic systems of government, (d) the changing needs of the workforce, (e) a changing view of the role of government and the capacity of government to solve problems, and (f) a new understanding of what is basic. These are worth examining because they suggest how changes in the broader society may affect schooling.

Increased Valuing of the Individual

It is interesting to speculate about the reasons underlying the growing emphasis on the value of the individual. Smaller family size and lower infant and child mortality rates led parents to value each child more and to appreciate each child's individual characteristics. The increasing education level of each succeeding generation created a stronger sense of individualism. Individuals are being called upon to make increasingly complex decisions. The actions of each individual have more impact within families, organizations, and society generally.

The increasing emphasis on the individual holds the potential to be both a blessing and a curse. If American schools continue to be places in which students are not able to develop as individuals, many more will lose interest in schooling. Factory models of schooling likely will not be successful as a means to develop key skills for the future, such as teamwork and quality work. Many schools have a long way to go to become places in which the educational program takes students' individuality into account.

More recently, the emphasis on the individual has begun to swing back in the direction of individual responsibility for one's actions. Schools profess to believe in this value and to develop it. Can schools become places in which students take responsibility for their actions, where they feel they have had some choice about what they do and how they act, so they can be responsible for their choices?

The Triumph of the Marketplace

The triumph of the marketplace worldwide affirms a preference for individual decisions over the forces of bureaucracy. In marketplace economies, it is the decisions of individuals that determine prices, products, markets, jobs, and even the makeup communities. Marketplace societies abhor faceless bureaucracies.

Whether this is how free market economies actually operate is not the point. What matters is the perception in much of the world that such a system provides the best hope for individual and collective prosperity. This is particularly important for educators to consider because two key elements of the marketplace philosophy, choice and competition, are troublesome to public education.

Educators can expect policymakers to explore the concepts of choice, competition, and deregulation as possible remedies for the ills of public education. These remedies have been applied during the past decade to such protected sectors of the economy as airlines, trucking, hospitals, and telephone companies; and these were businesses that were doing well in delivering their services! After nearly a decade of more or less nonstop criticism of public education, and little in the way of concrete improvement from the perspective of policymakers and the public at large, pressure is mounting to try something more radical to reshape education. Given the symbolic power of the free market, policymakers may look toward choice and competition as concepts to "rescue" public education. Educators may need to consider how to incorporate these values into the existing school system so that it can evolve from a bureaucracy to something that is more market-driven, or at least market-sensitive.

The Rise of Democracies

The triumph of the marketplace and the growth of democratic institutions goes hand in hand in many parts of the world. However, the spread of democracy worldwide has some unintended implications for schools. Democracies are based on the participation and consent of the governed. In democratic societies, these principles are often applied to work settings and even schooling. Because schools often must rely on some degree of coercion, such as mandatory attendance or discipline codes, they run counter to the values of a democracy in some ways. Although the public often supports strict discipline in schools, if schools become too heavy-handed, they run the risk of alienating parents. Only recently have teachers and parents been invited to participate in decision making in many schools. In democracies, participation and consent are key principles. Will schools be able to adopt these principles?

When educators step back and examine their current practices, they may realize that they are focused on developing a "perfect" attendance or discipline system rather than on how to engage students actively in their education or how to enlist parents and community members as equal partners in education. The inconsistencies become clearer when students and parents demand greater involvement in decisions. Members of society expect participatory decision making and democracy, but schools appear not to support this principle.

The Influence of Workforce Needs

As noted earlier, the influence of the business community on educational restructuring is substantial. Whether one believes that business should influence educational programs or not, there is no denying the influence that various business-related groups have had in shaping the restructuring agenda. To understand how the business community's need for greater economic productivity and adaptability is translated into calls for educational reform, it is useful to consider three key documents that outline what business believes students should be able to know and do.

In 1990, the Commission on the Skills of the American Workforce published *America's Choice: High Skills or Low Wages.* American workers, the report says, are at a crossroads: They must develop higher skills to produce goods with high value on the international market or else face decreasing wages as they compete with low-wage, Third World workers in the production of low-value, mass-produced items.

A second report, which also has been widely circulated among educators, indicates more specifically the types of skills that employers desire in employees in the 1990s. Titled *Workplace Basics: The Skills Employers Want* and produced jointly by the American Society of Training and Development and the U.S. Department of Labor's Employment and Training Administration, the report was the result of interviews with employers throughout the nation.

A third report that has also been reviewed and discussed by many school faculties, superintendents, boards of education, state legislators, and departments of education interested in reform was commissioned by the U.S. Department of Labor and titled *What Work Requires of Schools: A SCANS Report for America 2000.* It identifies five competencies and a three-part foundation of skills and personal qualities that the commission described as necessary "for solid job performance."

I find in these reports some possible agreement between what the business community says it wants from workers and what many parents and educators want in a well-educated person. Both groups tend to want the following for students:

- A curriculum that emphasizes problem solving, application, and integration of knowledge and higher-order thinking over rote learning and memorizing facts
- Opportunities for students to actively engage in learning, not merely follow directions
- Learning that is measured in terms of the ability to do something, not the amount of time spent in a seat
- Education that extends beyond the walls of the classroom into the larger community and the workplace
- Teachers who help create lifelong learners, who develop a student's learning skills, and are not content merely to transmit a body of information; teachers who help instill a love of learning in students
- Chances for students to work in groups and as members of teams
- Schooling that reaches every student and that produces young adults with positive self-images and the ability to define goals for themselves
- The belief that all students can learn

A Changing View of the Role of Government and Its Ability to Solve Problems

The mid-1990s is a time of redefinition. As the economy continues to redefine itself as a part of a global network of goods and services, and as society seeks to understand how to function with new family structures and changing definitions of community, the role of government is also undergoing close scrutiny. The public appears to have less faith in government. There is more cynicism about politicians and political institutions. Fewer people believe that government is a compact among people to solve problems that cannot best be solved by individuals.

Furthermore, most governmental units—national, state, or local—are broke or close to it. They have reached the limits of what the public appears willing to pay as taxes. This is due in part to the fact that the real income of the middle class has not been growing much for the past 15 years. Those middle-class people who have more money generally have it because they are working more hours, or have family members who have entered the workforce to raise family income. Taxpayer revolts are commonplace. Government cannot solve problems by spending more money on them.

Many of the social programs that have come into existence over the past 60 years are being reexamined. The notion that any social issue should be addressed by government is being questioned by both political parties. Although trends like this ebb and flow, this movement to reexamine big government is already 15 years old and is continuing to gain momentum. At least for the foreseeable future, it seems likely that there will be many elected officials at all levels of government committed to decreasing the role of government, or of examining, eliminating, or redesigning many long-standing social programs. Public schools are the largest governmental agency in most states. They have been asked to take on many roles. These roles are likely to be closely reexamined.

A New Understanding of What Is Basic

In the past, it seemed fairly easy to discern what "the basics" were. Everyone needed to be able to read, write, and calculate. Spelling and grammar were useful, as was some geography and history, a basic sense of science, maybe a bit of literature, and a dab of music or art.

Although there are certainly many who advocate roughly that curriculum today, the definition of today's basics is quite different. The level of education that is expected of all citizens is indicated quite clearly in a number of tasks that almost everyone must master at some point in their lives. Several examples serve to illustrate just how much education we expect (or demand) people to have if they are to be successful in our society.

Everyone pays taxes, or at least most everyone completes the beloved 1040 form. Most people dread it, to the point where whole industries have sprung up simply to fill out these forms for people. The tax system is structured to benefit those who are able to decrease the amount of money upon which they are taxed by itemizing allowable deductions and other expenses. As anyone knows who has attempted this process, once you begin to itemize, the complexity of the process increases dramatically.

Certainly, it is quite possible to rely on a trained professional to handle these tasks. I am not saying everyone should be taught to complete 1040s. However, taxpayers benefit by understanding how the tax code works, in broad terms. It is not enough to be able to add and subtract. It is not enough to be able to fill in the boxes on the return. Citizens as taxpayers need a deeper understanding of what they should do throughout the year to reduce taxes, and how they should communicate with a trained person about the decisions they have made.

Have you tried to buy a house or car or to refinance a mortgage lately? These activities used to be fairly straightforward. Now the choices are nearly limitless: Fixed term, variable; own, rent, lease; low down payment, high down payment, no down payment; effects on taxes, future capital gains, and so on. Once again, the problems here are not primarily addition and subtraction (although a calculator with an amortization function is quite handy), but rather the basic strategy one chooses to pursue and the numerous implications of one choice or another. I would not downplay the importance of good computational skills here or elsewhere, but they alone don't help you decide whether to take a 5-year adjustable rate mortgage with a 6 point cap over a 30-year fixed mortgage with lower closing costs. These major life decisions—buying a home or automobile—have become hopelessly complex. Little of what students are taught prepares them to handle these key events.

How about employment? One of the fastest growing sources of jobs is entrepreneurial activities; in other words, businesses that people start themselves. What knowledge and skill does it take for a person to start his or her own business? A careful analysis and listing is very informative. To be successful, an entrepreneur would need to be able to develop a business plan, pursue financing, locate a physical site, advertise, deal with numerous governmental and quasi-governmental agencies, keep myriad records and make reports, and comply with applicable laws. On top of that, today's entrepreneurs must be adaptive and aware of the market and their niche. They must be able to manage people successfully and to understand the concept of quality. They must be good communicators, both oral and written.

Many students from historically blue-collar backgrounds have been able to start businesses in America. Fewer of them will attempt to do so, or succeed, if they do not have the skills outlined above. Starting a small trucking business should be an option for many since the deregulation of trucking over the past 15 years. However, to do so requires computer skills; knowledge of hazardous materials transit regulations; accounting skills; and an understanding of workman's compensation, unemployment, Social Security, and Medicare regulations. How many working-class kids have a realistic shot at setting up their own businesses with the education they now receive?

There's one last example to consider. Do you live in a state that employs the initiative? Even if you don't, there are numerous elections in your community on a multitude of topics. Examine the types of issues on which the public in your state or community is being asked to make major decisions. Are you satisfied that their education prepared them to make such decisions? As we move decision making more and more into the public arena, isn't it reasonable to expect that the education that students receive is commensurate with the complexity of the issues they are being asked to decide? Can a democracy function successfully with citizens making decisions they are not prepared to make? Read the voter's pamphlet in your city or state and think about which skills and knowledge citizens need to make the decisions they are being called upon to make.

A curriculum that prepared all students to do the things listed above would be quite different from today's. This is where the call for restructuring comes from; the realization that the match between what people actually must do during their lives and the education they receive to prepare them is grossly out of sync.

The View From Other Agencies and Teachers

The rationale for restructuring emanates from many sources: from changes in families and society; from the economy, both domestically and internationally; from the changing face of technology and its awesome potential to transform learning; and from changes in the learners themselves. Although the business community has so far been the clearest and most consistent in its call for fundamental educational reform, there are many others who advocate changes in schooling, even if they are not aware that they are doing so.

Social service agencies, local and state governments, and juvenile justice and police departments all recognize the degree of alienation present among many of today's young people. These agencies also deal with the traumas and tragedies that occur all too frequently in many families. Among personnel in these agencies, there is a growing awareness that schools are going to have to be closer partners with parents and community agencies if the next generation of young people are going to be brought to maturity with the attitudes and behaviors necessary to be successful citizens.

Educators themselves often possess the clearest understanding of the need to change schooling drastically. They are overburdened by demands on them that they cannot possibly meet: to be teachers, social workers, surrogate parents, advisors, mentors, disciplinarians, and a host of other roles. They must see too many students for too short of a time. They work in places that often resemble factories from the 1930s or before. Their students often arrive exhausted because their jobs kept them up until midnight each school night. They may have students coming and going all year long. Those who are there may be unruly. Materials are often inadequate or nonexistent.

In the face of such a scenario, many teachers give up, in a sense. They do the best they can, or they go through the motions. They know there is little hope of solving these problems through the only solution that seems possible to them, namely, a large increase in funding. For these teachers, their jobs are all the more difficult because there is no improvement in sight, nor is any ever likely to appear.

Other educators who know full well the importance of adequate funding also appreciate the need to change the structure of schooling if any lasting improvement is to occur. They understand that investing more and more resources in structures that can never adequately meet the new demands for schooling will only lead inevitably to frustration and failure. They advocate a rethinking of the basic assumptions, practices, and structures of schooling. They believe it is time to go back to the basics by questioning everything about schools and schooling that has not been seriously questioned in this century.

For serious change to occur in a school, there must be a strong rationale for it. One of the first things that any school considering restructuring should do is determine the rationale for changing, then see if staff and community accept that rationale. If they don't, it is almost certainly time either to rethink the rationale or to work with both to deepen their understanding and acceptance of the rationale for restructuring.

DISCUSSION QUESTIONS

1. In our school, what is the range of beliefs about the need to change schooling?

2. Are there any examples of how the school has become out of sync with the needs of students, employers, and society generally?

3. What examples are there of teachers doing an outstanding job to meet student needs? In what way does the current structure of schooling help them? Hinder them?

4. Are the forces over which educators have no control so powerful that there is little likelihood that schools and schooling will ever be redesigned to meet the needs of today's more demanding students?

5. Of the six changes in values outlined in the chapter, which can be observed in your state? In your community? What are some examples of how these values affect educational policy and decisions?

6. What role should the needs of business play in determining changes to be made in this school?

7. Should restructuring wait until adequate resources are available? What constitutes adequate resources? When might these be available?

3 *Fundamental Beliefs and Assumptions*

Although schools profess to be "neutral" on issues of values and morals, all schools must have an underlying set of values and morals. Things like honesty, hard work, consideration, and courtesy are examples, and there are many others. These values generally mirror the community in which the school exists. This makes perfect sense. However, what happens when communities do not agree about their values and moral systems? The compass does not point north with consistency. What are schools to do in an environment of conflicting signals?

Furthermore, what should schools do if some of the community's values could be harmful to many students? How can educators and community members determine if the root cause of some problem is a deeply held belief (or pathology) in the community? They can start by asking themselves what their fundamental beliefs and values are, particularly as they relate to education. Asking people to examine assumptions long untested is particularly difficult, but important, at this point in history if a school proposes to modify any of its basic practices or structures.

I offer the following examples of new assumptions that challenge existing, commonly held beliefs about schools, schooling, and learning. They suggest new structures and methods based on new values. These provide a departure point for a school's discussion of its own beliefs and values.

1. *Essentially all students can be educated to some relatively high level of functioning.*

In the past, schools were expected to help a few students to reach high levels or to ensure that everyone was treated more or less the same. There is every indication that schools are now being expected to address both excellence and equity simultaneously, that schools will be expected to educate essentially all students to a high level.

Exactly what is meant by a high level is only now being defined. It is clear, however, that high school dropout rates of 25% will not be acceptable, nor will rates of 20%, 15%, or even 10% in the long run. Schools in the past have been more concerned with sorting students than with educating everyone. It will no longer be sufficient merely to keep students in school, to "warehouse" them until they are old enough to work. How will schools retain and educate all students without creating "winners" and "losers"?

For starters, the notion that intelligence is distributed throughout the population in a way best described by a bell-shaped curve will have to be challenged. As long as this assumption is accepted as the basis for educational practice, there will be winners and losers *by definition.* Much of generally accepted educational practice is based on this deep, unspoken, unquestioned assumption. Practices such as tracking, standardized testing, grading on a curve, talented and gifted, and remedial education are all based on the notion that any group of students can be distributed into a few who are bright, a large group who are unexceptional but capable, and a small group who are simply not very able.

A number of other nations have educational systems in which the vast majority of students do reach some reasonably high level of performance. Certainly, some do better and some do worse. But ability is not spread along a continuum; performance is clustered more toward the top of the scale. If some national systems of education can do this, then it presents an alternative to the notion of the normal distribution, or at least calls into question the level of performance that most students are capable of achieving in public education.

2. *Learning is what students can do at the conclusion of education, not simply the processes in which they have participated.*

Education is currently measured in terms of the time spent in each learning experience. Students progress yearly by age group in elementary school and accumulate credits, or units, based on the time spent in each secondary school class. Credits in high school are expressed in terms of Carnegie units. The Carnegie unit was established early in the 20th century to ensure consistency and to institute some form of quality control among high schools for the purpose of college admissions. The Carnegie unit guaranteed that all students spent the same amount of time studying any subject for which they received credit. It did not address performance— what students could do after spending that time in a classroom. Now the emphasis has shifted from the time spent in class to what the student is able to do.

Such a shift implies that the school will be organized in ways that allow students more time and support when necessary to succeed. It further requires that the standards for success be clearly identified, along with the means of assessing performance. Currently, individual teachers devise grading systems and apply them in the absence of any overall standards. Some systems measure performance, attitude, attendance, improvement, or a combination of all. Performance-based systems require clear standards consistently applied and adequate opportunities for students to meet the standards.

3. *Education has economic utility for essentially all students and for society.*

Educators often question those who state that the primary purpose of an education is to prepare students for the workforce. Many, perhaps most, educators believe that education has goals other than preparing people for employment, and that public schools should maintain a healthy distance from business.

Without arguing the relative merits of this perspective, educators generally acknowledge that education plays a critical role in determining their students' economic future. Gone are the days when a student could drop out of high school and enter a high-paying career-track job. Given this reality, the linkage between the realities of the economy and the structure, content, and outcomes of a public education is becoming tighter. One can argue the appropriateness of this linkage. However, it appears that this trend will continue for the foreseeable future, in part because education, in the form of training and retraining, is becoming such an integral part of the workplace. Knowing how to learn will be as important as the specific factual information one possesses.

4. Learners participate actively in their own education in a variety of ways. learning cannot be passive.

One often hears from teachers and administrators that today's students are not like those in previous generations. Although this lament can be traced back literally thousands of years, today's educators may be accurate, in part because the way children are raised has indeed changed—and in part because schools have not.

Today's student must be motivated in different ways from children whose parents supported the school without reservation. In the 1950s, when corporal punishment was much more common, it would not be unusual for a student to receive a whack at school, notify his parent of the event, and receive two more at home. Fast-forward to the 1990s. If a student now notifies his parent of a teacher touching the child, let alone spanking him, the parent's response might be: "Call the lawyer!"

Students with clear sights on a college education still seem willing to do what is asked of them, largely without questioning. This creates the illusion for teachers that the system could still work, if only the other students had the same "right" attitude. In the meantime, the vast majority of the students may just be "going through the motions," doing as little as possible, frustrating teachers, and creating discipline problems. Kids from non-middle-class backgrounds may be among the least motivated, but even "good" suburban schools see this pattern. In effect, many children receive a minimal level of learning because they are not motivated to do the things that teachers ask. They can see no reason to comply, other than if the student likes the teacher or is interested in what is being taught.

Many of the things that kids are asked to do are not very interesting or useful. Grades may be a measure of compliance and cooperation with the teacher rather than a determination of learning. Even when grades are based on student achievement, the learning tasks judged are often repetitive, monotonous, uninspiring, or confusing. When students ask why they need to learn something, the most common answer is, "You need this to go to college." Sometimes this is true; sometimes not. In either case, it does not do much to excite or challenge most students.

Schools should engage students actively while maintaining high standards. These are difficult goals to achieve. Active participation in learning is achieved by having individual goals and strategies for students and more instructional techniques that actively involve students, such as project-centered learning, inquiry learning, simulations, cooperative and team learning, apprenticeships, internships, and real-world experiences.

Teachers become diagnosticians and planners, tailoring and modifying educational experiences to student needs and interests. Schools adapt many practices to accommodate active learning, including time, curriculum, location of learning experiences, and methods of assessing.

This is not an argument for permissiveness, lowered standards, or a "do-your-own-thing" educational experience akin to the 1960s. To the contrary, educational programs that engage students actively are more demanding for both teachers and students. They require more hours, more work of a higher quality, and more accountability than many current classrooms, which feature endless worksheets, unchallenging reading assignments, and irrelevant tests. In environments where students are actively engaged, teachers are not the primary motivators of students' performance. Instead, their energy is magnified by the inherent interest in the tasks and activities that students are asked to do. Teachers serve as catalysts who energize learners as the learners engage in interesting, meaningful tasks.

5. *Education is a responsibility that extends beyond schools: Parents, employers, and community members have responsibilities for the education of the community's young, along with a right to be included as partners in important decisions about education.*

As mentioned in the previous section, educators and policymakers alike agree on the need for a renewed partnership between schools and the broader community. Schools now have many safeguards, legal and otherwise, against those parents or interest groups that would abuse teachers or schooling. The challenge now is to create a new balance between the professional responsibilities and authority of educators and the inherent rights of parents and community members to see that their children receive a quality education.

Some educators note that many communities are laden with pathologies—abusive parents, drugs, crime, and lack of respect for authority. Other educators point to their communities and warn of obsessive parents who push their children to achieve, of parents who bear grudges against schools generally, of special interest groups supporting any number of programs, and of a majority that cares little about what happens in school as long as kids are kept off the street. The degree to which these perceptions are accurate varies considerably from community to community. These problems are very real. At the same time, the potential for positive community relations is always there, even in the most difficult settings. Many adults

in any community do care about the well-being of children, and they should
be given the opportunity to assist the school. Assuming that the community
cannot or should not be involved with the school is probably a mistake.

The community needs to have some ownership in the school's goals.
Involving parents and community in goal setting is only a first step. The
community then must be kept informed of progress toward achieving the
goals and have the means to influence the strategies used to achieve the
goals. Schools will need to be less afraid to acknowledge when goals are
not adequately achieved and to publicize any shortfall as a challenge to the
entire community.

Community means more than parents. Employers are beginning to
perceive a direct link between education and productivity. They are willing to do more than simply donate money. Some are providing opportunities for young people to understand more about the world of work and
the skills required to function successfully in the job market after graduation.

In an increasingly complex world where resources for education are
likely to remain relatively constant, partnerships between schools and other
segments of society can help keep education relevant and exciting for
students. Those partnerships can also improve support for public education
at a time when fewer than 25% of families have children in school.

6. *Schools may be the only place where a sense of genuine community can
be developed for young people. They might better function more like communities than factories.*

As many neighborhoods continue to crumble, educators face (at least)
two choices. They can (a) lament the decline of support for education from
home and community and wash their hands of the responsibility to educate
students who do not come to school with the desired background and
attitudes; or (b) accept that schools may be the only place in the student's
life where he or she is safe, valued, and supported. If educators accept the
second option, they must redesign schools so that they reflect the needs
that students have to feel a sense of belonging and value as individuals.

If educators accept that the first option is self-defeating, they will want
to determine if their school is a genuine and healthy community for young
people. In many cases, what they will discover may not be pleasant. The
basic design of today's schools comes from an era when students were
expected to have many more of their needs met in the community; in their

extended family; church; and in various social activities, such as 4-H, Boy Scouts/Girl Scouts, religious groups, or ethnic organizations. In many cases, these institutions no longer exist. Youth are left to identify with the mass culture created by retailers and the media or, of greater concern, with gangs or cliques that embrace antisocial values. Kids are driven by a need to belong. If they can't find it at home, at school, or in the community, they will find it elsewhere.

Part of the problem is that there are fewer positive adult role models for young people. The problem is worse in large schools, where a child can attend several years and be known by only a handful of acquaintances and teachers. They develop few relationships with adults who can show them how to behave. Such schools create conditions that support increased alienation and decreased success. Not only are the young deprived of role models, they spend most of their time with other children almost exactly their own age, and are, in effect, socialized by their peers. They have few role models of any sort other than kids their own age, which is a scary thought.

One strategy is to restore schools to a human scale. How "economical" is it really to house 2,000 students in one building if hundreds of them are dropping out each year, at least in part due to feelings of alienation and a sense that no one cares about them? Each of them represents not only lost opportunities but lost funding for the school.

Schools may need to become places where many adults interact with a modest number of students (perhaps 150 to 300). Adults can participate in roles other than teachers, as volunteers, mentors, observers, tutors, "counselors," or resource people. Adults can mean college students to retired people. Students can develop a healthier identity and stronger affiliation with the school by interacting and developing relationships with competent, healthy adults and with a wider range of young people. Students are then not as subject to the demands of the peer group. They feel part of a large group and can explore different behaviors, knowing what socially appropriate behavior looks like.

These six new "habits of heart and mind" illustrate changes that educators may need to make in their underlying assumptions, given changes that have already occurred in society. As people in a school change their assumptions, it becomes much easier to make changes in the school. This is so because people come to see and accept the need for change more clearly. Energy then can be focused primarily on making new approaches work, rather than on fighting battles about the need for change.

DISCUSSION QUESTIONS

1. What are the key current fundamental beliefs and assumptions operating in this school?

2. Can all students actually be educated to a high level?

3. What are the conditions that are necessary if this is to occur?

4. What is the proper role of an education in preparing students for the world of work?

5. Does the school's current instructional program engage students actively? How? To what degree?

6. How do parents and community members perceive their involvement in the school currently? What would happen if expectations for them changed?

7. In what ways is this school a community?

PART II

What Does
Restructuring
Look Like?

4 *Educational Standards and Assessment*

The Role of Educational Standards

Perhaps the single most significant educational issue before the nation currently is whether students should be judged on their ability to reach defined performance standards, and whether schooling should be organized around such standards. The debate is complex, confusing, and often highly charged. Given the magnitude and implications of this proposed change, such reactions should not be surprising.

Why Standards?

Why is there a need to have clearly defined standards in schools today? Isn't it clear what kids need to know? Don't schools already know this? Why go to all the trouble of setting standards?

There are at least two reasons. First, it is becoming more and more difficult to agree on the "common" standards for schooling. As America becomes more diverse, there is a wider range of opinions within any given community of what students need to know and be able to do. It cannot be assumed that everyone agrees what the standards are or should be.

It's also less clear that the standards that were in place 40, 50, or 60 years ago are the right ones for today. Those standards worked in part because students who did not meet them simply did not continue in school. As recently as 1953, the high school graduation rate was 50%. Half of the students had left by the time they were 17. The standards of the 1950s worked—for about half the students.

What Do We Mean by "Standards"?

So many different terms have been used and interpretations offered that it's not entirely clear what people mean when they talk of "standards." To some, this means "outcomes." Outcomes, in turn, mean different things to different people. Some see outcomes as value-laden tools that take control of education away from parents and local communities. Others see them as vehicles for defining in general terms the skills and abilities that students will need in the future. The two sides have not tended to communicate well with one another, leading to emotional exchanges about "outcomes-based education" that echo earlier reactions in the 1970s to programs like "values clarification."

At the heart of the matter is a relatively simple principle upon which all sides seem to agree: American students should be held to higher standards than they are currently, and these standards should be stated clearly. Beyond this, there is less agreement. Some want a clear focus on "the basics." Others contend that there are the "old basics" and the "new basics." Some believe that if the state specifies outcomes, it will dictate how students are to think. Others believe students need to know clearly what is expected of them in school, both in terms of what they are to learn and how they are to behave; that many children are being raised in homes where there is less attention to values than in previous generations; and that schools have little choice but to instill some values in order to maintain order in the classroom.

The differences apparently center on some basic definitions, values, and views about students as learners. Opponents to "outcomes-based education" often express concerns about a range of instructional strategies and programs such as whole language, cooperative learning, interdisicplinary teaching, values education, and a variety of techniques that have gained popularity during the past 25 years. The term "New Age" is often applied broadly by opponents to a range of teaching methods and curricular programs. The more extreme opponents see international conspiracies lurking in "outcomes-based education" that are intended to control the minds of our youth.

Proponents of standards argue that they are not advocating any particular teaching strategy, but a system that requires essentially all students to reach specified levels of performance. To do so, expectations must be stated clearly, and a variety of support structures must be in place to help those students who need additional time to reach the identified performance level. Proponents generally argue for both lower level (factual) knowledge, and higher level (cognitive) skills.

Opponents of standards worry that the standards will lower expectations. How can a standard be set high enough, they ask? Won't it have to be set as a "lowest-common denominator?" Many seem to believe that educators are inherently motivated to lower standards within education. They are wary of assessment schemes, such as portfolios of student work or public demonstrations by students, that they view as more subjective than standardized tests. Some feel very strongly that standards are a smokescreen for enforcing a common set of state-prescribed values on all young people. They state emphatically that the standards are not clear enough, and the content that students will master is not specified in adequate detail. Will students have to know their multiplication tables and when the Civil War took place? Or will they simply have to be able to "think," or "interpret human experience"?

At the heart of the difference between opponents and proponents may be their attitude about the type of changes needed in education generally. Many opponents believe education needs to become more like it used to be, when there was a clear core of basic skills that students learned in school, and the family, church, and community were responsible for the remainder of the child's education. Schools got into trouble, they argue, when they strayed from their core mission and took on roles better left to the family and community. Standards are seen as one more tentacle, one more attempt by government to get into the lives of citizens when it does not belong there.

Religious groups have equally strongly held beliefs. Some religious groups have more diffuse concerns. They lump in outcomes-based education with a long list of other things about which they have concerns, such as visualization, meditation, values clarification, organizational visions, mission statements, and, in some cases, older issues such as sex education or evolution. Their basic concern seems to be that these techniques and others like them promote a form of worship that they deem blasphemous. They see these techniques, and many others, as direct threats to Christian values and Christian families.

Proponents contend that schools never did meet the needs of all students, and that educational standards help address the very concerns about lowered expectations that critics voice. Proponents believe that communities, families, and students themselves need greater guidance from schools about what students must know and be able to do to succeed in society. Most proponents would agree that all students will not reach high standards without parents and other adults being actively engaged in the child's education. They see standards as a way to engage these adults actively by making clear to them what their students must do to succeed.

Proponents are often deeply puzzled and offended when they are attacked by opponents, sometimes in the strongest and most personal forms imaginable. The proponents often agree with many of the concerns that the opponents have about the educational system, but for some reason are unable to communicate this shared sense of concern to them. The dialogue and communication has broken down completely in many communities.

There is a third group with concerns about outcomes-based education, those parents who believe that this approach has not been proven as an educational strategy and worry that their children are being used as guinea pigs in some grand educational experiment. These parents, along with community members who share their concerns, raise many questions when outcomes-based education programs are proposed in a community. Where is the guarantee that this method is better than what they are doing now?

This debate is not likely to be resolved in an amicable fashion anytime soon. At the same time, American schools seem unable to achieve anything other than very small incremental gains in student learning. Is it time to look at strategies such as standards that would transform the learner's responsibilities and increase educator accountability, or are standards too politicized an issue currently? Schools that proceed without standards will be challenged to show how they can improve student learning with the current system and (probably) fewer resources. Implementing standards, a potentially powerful tool for focusing student and teacher efforts, threatens the natural tendency of schools to avoid controversy.

Given the contentious nature of anything that could be associated with outcomes-based education, how should a school respond to the need for standards in a school district when it is clear that no program of restructuring is likely to succeed if it is not focused on students achieving high standards? There are several issues that probably should be considered. First, to what degree are there standards already in place in the school, and to what degree do these standards drive student performance? Some schools have created strong cultures of achievement with clear, high, consistent standards. These schools have long employed a variety of assessment methods and have a history of advertising student performance to the community. Such environments, although the exception, probably need only examine national standards documents and applicable state standards and incorporate them into their curriculum, instruction, and assessment practices.

Within schools, many programs have always used standards in some form. Many vocational education classes use competencies, specific statements of what a student must learn to progress through the program. These are a form of outcomes. Similarly, some programs of reading and mathematics instruction move students lesson by lesson through very clear tasks and skills that must be acquired before the student moves on. This is the principle of outcomes broken down into its most basic form. It is found in programmed instruction packages used in computer labs and so-called "integrated learning systems." Home economics, wood shop, metals, and electronics have always identified the skills that students must master, then judged them on the "outcomes" of their work.

Even in extracurricular areas, the principles of standards-based education are frequently found. Science fairs have criteria against which projects are judged. These are standards. Similarly, speech and debate tournaments, and programs for the talented and gifted, such as Odyssey of the Mind, judge student work against standards. Students know these standards as they prepare to compete, and they know they must meet them. Different students take differing amounts of time to prepare, but in the end, all are judged against the same standards.

The only place where clear standards do not appear with much frequency is within core academic programs: English, mathematics, science, social studies, and foreign languages. In these subjects, students attend class regularly, do assignments, and take tests. The exception is courses such as Advanced Placement, where students prepare for a specific test that is scored externally. Student performance in core academic subjects is judged by individual teachers with individual grading standards based on individual preferences, skills, interests, and, in some cases, prejudices. These individual systems may or may not reflect student knowledge and skills, as any parent who has had problems with a particular teacher's grading system will attest.

When there is agreement that standards are needed to boost student performance, the first issue will likely be: How should they be developed and agreed upon? The most immediate issue will be to ensure that every voice in the community is heard early and throughout the process. It will be equally important to establish a balance within the standards between content knowledge and more general, overarching cognitive, intellectual, and social skills. In general, the more concern in the community about outcomes, the closer to recognized content disciplines the standards should adhere.

This is not to suggest that even in such communities, standards need to be confined to "basic skills" or lower-order thinking. In fact, there are numerous examples of school districts and state systems of education that have begun to produce standards systems based on challenging content that also integrate desirable "process" skills, such as writing, problem solving, and quality work. What is important is that the standards and the rationale for the inclusion of each is clearly understood by the community. Furthermore, each standard should be teachable and testable in a way that the community (and teachers and students) can comprehend.

Involving the community can be complicated and potentially contentious. A great deal of groundwork needs to be done. Care should be taken not to allow small extremist groups at either end of the spectrum to dominate the process. Final recommendations might best come from a "blue ribbon" commission of respected citizens and educators. Standards should be released in draft form and put into place on a trial basis to allow concerns to be identified and rectified quickly. At the same time, many patrons will become more educated about the content of the standards.

Whenever possible, a community's standards should refer or link to standards developed elsewhere. It makes little sense to reinvent the wheel completely. Furthermore, what is the point of developing standards that do not equip the student to succeed beyond the community? Many organizations are developing standards, including state departments of education, national curriculum organizations, credible national testing organizations such as The College Board and American College Testing, school districts, regional educational labs, and special projects such as New Standards. If the standards that a community adopts can be linked to other external groups, it is easier to show how students will be better prepared to succeed in the world at large.

There are other issues that must be addressed, including the concern that standards will be set at a "lowest common denominator" level to enable all students to succeed, and that the class will be held back waiting for the slowest student to reach a required level of performance. It is important to discuss and address issues such as these before standards are set. The school's design must demonstrate that having standards will not require teachers to use any particular instructional strategy, or will not require all students to wait while one student catches up. Parents need to know, and the school district needs to demonstrate, that the net effect will be increased performance and content knowledge for all students, and that many practices will be redesigned simultaneously to support a standards-based system.

There are trade-offs involved in adopting standards. Teachers cannot teach anything they please and evaluate what they teach against any standard they choose. In this sense, teacher autonomy is decreased. However, teacher professionalism is increased when teachers work together to ensure that students meet required standards. A standards-based system works best when teachers communicate with one another regarding what they are doing to prepare students to meet standards, and when information about student performance is available to teachers to enable them to plan better how to ensure that more students meet standards.

The goal of a standards-based educational system is increasing accountability for results while decreasing restrictions on how schools achieve the results. Teachers must be able to work together both to complement each others' efforts to make sure that students reach standards and to identify ways in which the educational environment, the classroom, and the school should be redesigned or adapted to help ensure that as many students as possible reach the standards.

Standards-based education, in the final analysis, is not any particular instructional methodology or curriculum. It is the commitment to establish a clear set of expectations for student performance, generally grounded in external standards and linked to challenging content, and to organize the school so that as many students as possible reach the standards. Some schools set the goal of having all students meet the standards. This noble goal is attainable, but not without allowing some students to demonstrate attainment of the standards in some modified or adapted form. Given this type of realistic approach to designing a standards-based system, schools can work to create instructional environments based on clear standards and high, challenging content.

Standards are at the heart of large-scale educational change. To adopt standards as the basic organizer for instruction and student progress is to commit to a series of other changes that will logically result. In the remainder of this chapter, I will outline some of the ways in which assessment may change if standards are instituted.

Changes in Assessing Student Learning

Standards and assessments are intertwined. A standard has no meaning without a way to assess whether or not it has been met. Similarly, assessments without standards, or external reference points, are meaningless. The term *assessment* has a range of meanings. I use it here to mean that there are a variety of ways in which achievement of a standard might be demonstrated. I distinguish between assessing and evaluating. To assess is to examine and analyze with the intention of determining worth; to evaluate is to make or reach a judgment. Both are important; however, evaluation in education at times has been less interested in worth and more concerned with judging. Assessment, as it is used here, refers to a variety of techniques for determining both the progress toward and the ultimate attainment of a standard by a student.

Once standards have been established, it is easier to determine what types of assessments are necessary and appropriate. Some standards essentially dictate the assessment. For example, a foreign language standard related to oral proficiency would strongly suggest an assessment where the student speaks the language. A writing standard probably requires a portfolio of student writing. Other standards are more difficult to assess. In the humanities, for example, assessing student mastery of literature can be achieved in many possible ways.

Assessments can provide useful information to teachers, students, and parents about performance relative to district or state standards, to district curriculum objectives, and to individual learner goals. Assessments that are linked to standards can easily provide comparisons among students for those parents who wish for, require, or demand such information. These requests are quite justifiable. In fact, if a district seeks to abandon standardized testing, it should be ready to provide some form of credible comparative data to parents in place of these tests.

If standards take hold in American education, assessment methods will have to undergo a drastic transformation from the limited assortment of multiple-choice tests and fill-in-the-blank methods used currently. The familiar saying "What gets measured gets done" applies. If students are to meet demanding standards that go beyond rote memorization, teachers will have to use assessments that prepare students for the standards.

Current testing methods will likely undergo considerable change. Most teacher-designed and standardized achievement tests seek to determine student knowledge about factual information and basic applications of principles or procedures. Methods such as a spelling test, math problems list, multiple-choice test in history, matching terms and definitions in science, and fill-in-the-blank in reading are very efficient, but often miss much of what is taught and learned.

These methods break learning down into small measurable units, and assume that if the students can do the units, they can combine them into a whole. Sometimes this is true; more often than not, it isn't. Standardized achievement tests may have high reliability (that is, perform similarly in different situations) but low validity (they may not measure what those giving the test want to know about the learner). In other words, they tell us a great deal about things that may have very little to do with what students actually know and are able to apply, or what we want them to know and be able to do.

Furthermore, they may drive the curriculum in undesirable directions. Teachers, students, and parents come to think that acceptable scores on achievement tests mean that the student is well-educated. The makers of these tests will tell you that this is not what the scores mean. Nevertheless, communities and the media take them seriously because there are few other measures, and educators are under pressure to raise these scores. These tests provide little insight into how well students understand what they are taught, how well they retain it, how they use what they are taught in their lives, or how the different pieces of what they learn come together in their minds. In fact, there is ample evidence that test-taking ability significantly influences scores for individual students and groups of students.

If expectations for student learning shift from measuring what students can retain for short periods of time to demonstrating what they can do with what they know over longer time frames, assessment will have to shift or evolve accordingly. This process of developing new methods is still in its infancy and will take a number of years to mature. In the meantime, schools involved in restructuring will be hard pressed to demonstrate improvement as long as they use only standardized tests.

Many states, school districts, and schools are experimenting with new methods of assessment. At first, new assessments should not be used to decide whether students should be moved from grade to grade or should graduate, but as a source of information about how well a program or school is doing. The results serve to inform and shape improvement.

Over time, however, these assessments will have more effect on individuals. The idea of performance-based certificates, for example, assumes that students must demonstrate that they have met the standards before the certificate is awarded. This is a departure from diplomas, which students receive after accumulating a prescribed number of credits or units.

Assessments that determine if a student receives a certificate will need to be subjected to more scrutiny than will those that simply report on a school's performance.

Current teacher-designed testing systems rarely meet the rigorous criteria applied to assessments that have a great impact on students. This is unfortunate because these teacher-developed instruments are the most common method of assessment now in use. The grades that students receive based on these tests are used to determine promotion, college admission, scholarships, and any number of other important matters. When new methods of assessment are being reviewed for technical merit, they are never compared to the existing methods, but to idealized standards. If they were, almost every method of assessment that judges students in relation to clear external standards would be found technically superior to the tests employed by individual teachers. And yet teacher-developed evaluation applied independent of any standard other than the teacher's are fiercely defended, perhaps inadvertently, by those who oppose standards or new assessments.

These new assessments can and should be developed with teacher participation. In fact, teacher involvement can help improve the validity of an assessment by helping to identify early in the design process what needs to be assessed. Most of the new assessments being developed derive directly from teacher experiences with students in classrooms. This is a far cry from a standardized achievement test or the tests that accompany textbooks or other published materials. Those instruments often have little or no relation to what occurs in classrooms. New assessments are designed to create a much stronger link between what teachers teach, what students learn, and how progress or success is determined. Brief descriptions of several forms of assessment follow.

Examples of Assessment Methods

A portfolio is a collection of a student's work that indicates his or her progress and ultimate competency in relation to a set of standards. Portfolios are frequently employed in art and more recently in writing. They give the student, teacher, and parent a better perspective on the student's progress over time in an area of study. They are particularly useful in areas where a grade tells little about overall progress or quality. Portfolios are scored as a whole, although they may be rated on a number of separate factors. Most schemes for judging portfolios employ scoring guides, or rubrics. These guides specify a number of levels of performance with an accompanying description of each level. Raters then decide into which level the portfolio falls. The scoring guide contains specific descriptions of behaviors and evidence of performance that an observer can use to analyze and categorize the student's performance along a continuum, usually designated by a numeric scale of 1 to 5, with five representing the highest, most competent, and most complex level of performance. The raters also have available actual examples of student work for each of the levels. These "anchors" make it much clearer what a 4 is and how it is different from a 5 or a 3.

One of the advantages of this method is that it can be developed and applied by teachers. The behaviors identified as the focal point for observation in most scoring guides are ones that can be grasped relatively easily by educators, students, parents, and community members. They also can generate discussion about what it is students should know and at what levels and by what means they should demonstrate mastery of this knowledge. Scoring guides that are written in clear language can be distributed to parents so that they know more precisely what is expected of their children. The guide can be applied to preliminary drafts or be used throughout a course of study to provide formative feedback to the learner indicating clearly what he or she must do to improve performance. Such feedback can be more valuable and useful than a score of 64 or 72 on a test. The standard for success is identified before the fact, as well. A 3 on a scale of 1 to 5 might be designated as meeting the school's standards for mastery.

Portfolios of student work have been used in some states and school districts to gauge student growth, encourage student self-analysis, and help students to develop a sense of ownership and pride in their work. They have also been used to determine the overall performance of students within a state in a particular area of study, such as writing. Portfolios stimulate discussion among teachers of what is acceptable student work. The discussion focuses not on abstract notions, but on actual student work. The experience is a powerful source of professional development for the teacher, who rarely sees other students' work.

Another popular method is performance assessment. A performance assessment, as its name implies, is one where the student performs in some fashion to demonstrate knowledge and skills. Performances generally are most effective when the learning is viewed as a whole rather than as a series of parts. Performance assessment also uses scoring guides or rubrics.

Schools already assess performance in many areas, although they may not recognize it. Sports events like track are very good examples. Students compete against one another and as members of a team, but also attempt to set "personal bests" or to reach standards or goals they and their coaches have established. There are no scoring guides, but performance against standards takes place nonetheless.

Similarly, speech and debate tournaments or musical competitions are forms of performance assessment. Students are judged on their performance as a whole against clear standards. Other activities, such as yearbook, have elements of performance assessment in that there is a product to be judged. The standards are relatively clear, even if they are not stated explicitly. Even if students in the yearbook class receive an "A," their peers will judge them on the quality of the yearbook itself, as will the students themselves.

In all of these examples, a student knows the difference between receiving a grade for these activities (as in a yearbook class) and the actual quality of the performance. Which would you say they take more seriously, the grade or the performance? Which is the more powerful learning experience?

The preceding examples illustrate both issues and techniques in assessment. The process of developing new methods of assessment is complex, yet critical to the success of school restructuring. Without clearly defined standards and assessment methods, it will be difficult, if not impossible, to demonstrate whether students are learning more or not. Parents, policymakers, and the public at large want more, not less, accountability. If this trend holds true, schools will be expected to provide more and better evidence that students are meeting standards, and that the school is improving over time. New assessment methods can be powerful tools to help address these expectations.

DISCUSSION QUESTIONS

1. What are the standards currently in our school?

2. How do we know that students have met the standards?

3. What happens when students do not meet the standards?

4. How do these standards (or the school's curriculum and instructional program) help prepare students for the future?

5. What does the term *outcomes* mean in this school? This community? This state?

6. What does the term *standards* mean in this school? This community? This state?

7. What should the balance be between specific content knowledge and more general cognitive skills that cut across disciplines?

8. What effect on student performance might clear, consistent, high standards have?

9. How are/were the current standards set?

10. How is student performance assessed? Do the methods result in the desired student performances? If there is a lack of match, how does this show up in terms of student performance?

11. How does the state assessment program affect the school's instructional program? Is the state contemplating any changes?

12. How familiar are teachers and parents with some of the new types of assessment?

5 Changes in Curriculum and Instruction

$\mathbf{M}$eaningful, long-term change in education does not occur without curriculum reform and improved instructional methods. Underlying many of the changes in curriculum and instruction are different assumptions about how knowledge is best organized and how students learn. The traditional emphasis on content coverage and rote learning of basic skills is being replaced by more in-depth treatment of topics and a focus on higher-order thinking skills. Changes in curriculum are occurring in a number of areas, including

- Attempts to strike a new balance between depth versus coverage in the curriculum
- More school-based curriculum development
- Efforts to achieve greater balance between subject area content and intellectual processes through infusion of tasks that generate higher-level thinking
- Extensive experimentation with curriculum integration
- Changes in the role of the textbook
- The role of various national reports suggesting changes in particular subject areas or disciplines
- A complete redesign of what used to be called vocational education
- Challenges to the content and teaching methods employed in traditional core academic courses

Depth Versus Coverage:
The Role of Thinking in the Curriculum

Perhaps the largest change being proposed in curriculum restructuring is to focus on depth of understanding versus coverage of content. The current view of curriculum holds that students should be exposed to as much important information as possible. Teachers often talk of "covering" the curriculum, perhaps not noting that one definition of "to cover" is "to hide from sight." As long as a curriculum is designed to cover vast areas with little understanding, it will be very difficult to achieve the kinds of mastery of the material that may be crucial for success in both higher education and the world of work.

The debate over depth versus coverage begins with the crucial and controversial issue of what is worth knowing. Most districts have identified curriculum goals and sometimes "scope and sequence" charts that lay out the approved plan for what gets taught when. Many districts have curriculum guides, sometimes elaborate, that suggest (or mandate) how to present required material.

In practice, the taught curriculum rarely coincides very closely with these well-developed plans. Teachers create the curriculum in their classrooms. They tend to use textbooks or other commercially prepared material as their basic framework for instruction. Although there is nothing wrong with this practice, and many teachers supplement these materials extensively, teaching often becomes a race to "get through Chapter 26 by June 5."

Textbook producers are caught in a difficult situation. They must sell enough of their product to cover costs and make a profit, but must attempt to meet (or accommodate) the diverse curriculum goals established by the 15,500 school districts or 50 state departments of education. They can hardly be faulted if they include a little bit of everything. Textbook adoption committees often simply review a book to see if it covers the required objectives. Worse yet, there is evidence to suggest that some adoptions are made based on the number and quality of the pictures that the text contains.

Schools can have curricula that are inconsistent or contradictory from grade to grade, or from elementary to middle to high school. This helps explain why some topics are taught repeatedly (the definition of a noun, for example, may be taught in nearly every grade), and others are touched upon only briefly although they are crucial to understanding a field of study.

What is often compromised in this never-ending procession of isolated bits of information, rules, and events is the development of the student's worldview, of the ways in which the knowledge being taught fits together and how it applies beyond school. Educators are developing and using new curricula that not only transmit factual information but cause the student to link and explore both the information and the implications of it. In short, they are asking students to think about what they are learning and to formulate their learnings into perspectives that help them understand the world better.

The abilities to think critically, solve a problem, present a rationale for a choice, argue convincingly for a point of view, or research an issue are skills that have not necessarily been developed or tested extensively in most American schools. Some students, generally those who are college-bound, do receive a program of instruction that develops these abilities, and the highest achievers in any school demonstrate an impressive mastery of high-level thinking skills. The challenge is to extend aspects of this way of thinking and using knowledge to more students.

Curriculum Integration

Many schools are exploring and enacting curriculum integration, particularly in elementary schools, but with increasing frequency in middle and high schools. Curriculum integration occurs when one or more subject areas are combined. For example, humanities courses have long integrated writing, literature, and the fine arts. More novel combinations are possible as well. Science and social studies might be combined for a study of the effects of housing developments on quality of groundwater, or broader understandings about the social context of scientific discovery. In fact, teachers are becoming increasingly creative in their ability to integrate subject areas.

Curriculum integration allows for thematic teaching, in which a theme becomes the organizer for the curriculum. Themes provide a basis for several teachers to coordinate their efforts across subject areas or grade levels. Large groups of students can work collaboratively on large-scale projects, such as a mock archaeological dig or a recommendation for urban renewal. In such complex curricula, students divide the tasks among themselves, and several teams contribute ideas. Integration and thematic teaching also allow units of study that span several weeks or more, as opposed to daily or weekly lessons. These longer periods of time enable students to understand the basic content knowledge better and to think about what they are doing. Learning makes more sense to them, in part because it is not so fragmented, and because it is linked to some tangible activity or culminating project.

Curriculum integration is not without its problems, particularly in secondary schools. It generally requires collaboration between two or more teachers who are expert in specific content areas. They must cooperate to develop new materials and activities or translate an existing curriculum into an appropriate lesson format, plan or coordinate instructional activities, agree on what students will be expected to know from each subject and how it will be assessed, and, in some cases, teach together in the classroom.

Creating the conditions that support this level of collaboration requires many changes in most schools. Schedules must be altered so that teachers can plan together. Sometimes, longer periods of time for teaching have to be created. Physical arrangements can help or hinder such efforts. Most important, in secondary schools, integration requires teachers who are inclined to operate in close collaborative relationships and schools that support such relationships. This may be why more elementary schools have integrated curricula, because one teacher generally delivers most of the instructional program and can integrate without necessarily collaborating with another teacher. Elementary teachers are trained as generalists, whereas secondary teachers are content experts.

At the same time, integration is probably needed more at the secondary level because this is the point that curriculum fragmentation begins to occur in earnest. The best evidence of the effects of fragmentation on students is their inability (or unwillingness) to apply skills learned in one subject or class to other learning tasks. Just expect students to write in a science class or use math extensively in a social studies class to see the results. They are not incapable of doing so; they just have never been expected to do so. Curriculum integration supports the application of skills and knowledge across a range of learning situations, thereby increasing the development and retention of the skills and knowledge.

New Structures for Vocational Education

One area fully involved in curricular upheaval is vocational education and industrial arts. The traditional programs in areas such as business; home economics; wood, metal, and auto shop; electronics; and welding have been undergoing a transformation during the 1990s. Theirs is a challenge fundamentally different from that faced by core academic courses. Vocational/technical courses must transform themselves to survive; they are not able to adapt a little bit here and there. The challenge is not to develop an "improved" wood shop curriculum, for example, because the question is the relevance of the subject itself.

Business courses, with their traditional emphasis on training students to use office machines or to master typing and stenography, find themselves increasingly unable to keep pace with changes in workplace technology and procedures. Schools generally cannot provide students with the latest computers or new basic office equipment, such as sophisticated audio voice mail systems or computer networks.

A more fundamental problem is that the roles of workers and the nature of office jobs are changing so fast. Although it was once possible to train business students in the basic use of a typewriter and calculator; instruct them in dictation, shorthand, and bookkeeping; and teach them to write business letters and answer telephones, business teachers now find themselves confronting a workplace where secretaries are being replaced by "executive assistants" who are expected to solve problems and make decisions, where voice mail takes over for receptionists, where computers directly link executives and managers, and where a letter may be written and delivered without a secretary ever seeing it. These changing roles and technologies present profound challenges to traditional business teachers, some of whom continue to insist that students learn to type first on electric typewriters.

These teachers are rising to the challenge. They now offer basic instruction in word processing and spreadsheets (if on obsolete computers). They team with English teachers to offer "Business English," where students learn how to become better communicators by applying their skills to business situations. They offer similar applications of mathematics that go beyond the old "business math" or "consumer math," which were often simpler versions of traditional math courses. They also use curriculum integration and thematic teaching to increase student interest and retention.

But the most ambitious new programs work in partnership with businesses to create simulated office environments, either on or off campus, where students run mock businesses and learn the critical thinking and interpersonal skills demanded by the workplace today. Some schools go a step farther, bringing work into the school. They create a series of actual businesses where students learn and get paid. This is often done in close cooperation with local employers so that the school is not a competitor, but a provider of services not readily available locally. These programs develop entrepreneurial abilities, not just technical office skills. In fact, many schools now offer programs in entrepreneurship.

Students are provided more opportunities to see the world of work. They participate in "executive internships" that allow them to serve as interns to lawyers, architects, or other professionals and receive academic credit. "Shadowing" experiences allow students to spend a day or two in the workplace to learn more about a particular line of work.

Shop teachers have perhaps even a greater challenge than that faced by business teachers. Their classes often have been a refuge for students who do not perform well in traditional academic courses. "What will become of these students without the shop?" they ask.

Some schools are choosing simply to eliminate these programs rather than reform them. In other places, the shop teachers themselves are developing new curricula and being retrained to offer hands-on instruction that is academically challenging. "Applied academics" classes are one strategy for filling the gap between old shop programs and traditional academic curricula.

New programs abound. They explore production technologies, robotics, computers, food sciences, child development, and child care. One example in this area, "Principles of Technology," has been adopted widely as a replacement for shop programs. In this curriculum, students must master mathematical and scientific principles and apply them to technological problems. Students understand and apply knowledge in the same class. The class is academic and applied at the same time. A wider range of students works together in the same class. The boundaries between "academic" and "vocational" are broken down.

Home economics classes are changing by incorporating chemistry into lessons on cooking, or shifting to the study of sociology, families, and young children. They teach about early childhood education and, in an increasing number of high schools, offer day care on campus as a "lab" for students to apply their skills. The link between families and social service agencies is explored and better understood as the evolution of the family is examined. The effects of social and demographic trends on the family are explored.

One inevitable result of these curricular adaptations by vocational educators is an overlap between what they do and what is taught in the core academic subjects. Science and mathematics are taught in shop; writing is taught in business; sociology and psychology in home economics. How are issues of credit and curricular continuity resolved when this begins to occur? Which courses should count toward college admission? Particularly with the movement toward applied academic courses, the distinctions between academic and vocational, between core and elective, between thinking and doing, become much less clear.

Challenge for Traditional Core Courses

Those who teach mandatory courses, such as math, English, science, and social studies, find themselves in an awkward position. Because students must take these classes to fulfill college entrance requirements, students cannot express their dissatisfaction by declining to enroll. Consequently, it is not as easy to discern problems with these courses. At the same time, as their colleagues who teach electives begin to modify their programs, teachers in the academic core areas will be challenged as well.

The introduction of performance standards may be the factor that causes these courses of study to be redesigned. As noted earlier, when you have standards, you need not require specific courses. In fact, students can pursue any one of many paths to meet the standard, including learning the required material on their own. The monopoly of the required courses is broken. Furthermore, because taking a class is no longer synonymous with meeting a standard, students will be motivated to seek the learning experiences that help them meet the standard, rather than simply knocking off required courses.

In such an environment, extensive integration of curricula is not only possible but almost mandatory, particularly if the standards require higher level thinking and integration of knowledge. The net effect is to create a strong rationale for a core curriculum in which all students participate; no more "bonehead" math or English. All students would have more core learning experiences together if all were being judged by the same standards.

Traditional Courses and College Admission

The last line of legitimacy for academic courses is traditional college admissions requirements. These are indeed a formidable challenge for curriculum reformers because higher education is only now beginning to acknowledge the existence of educational restructuring.

Ironically, most colleges and universities would maintain that students come to them with a series of deficiencies. Such deficiencies include inflated grade point averages, inadequate content knowledge, poor writing and reasoning skills, minimal problem-solving abilities, little intrinsic motivation or initiative, and, apparently, little love of learning. The result is that students who should be able to succeed in college do not. They have been told in high school that they are doing adequate work and taking the proper courses, but find themselves ill prepared nonetheless.

A number of universities and colleges, as well as some state systems of higher education, are beginning to develop admission systems that accept students based on performance, not required courses. Will students who have to meet standards perform better in college? Are colleges ready to alter or abandon their reliance on the current admission measures of course title, Carnegie units, letter grades, and class standing and replace them with measures of student performance derived from high standards of content knowledge and cognitive skill? If colleges and universities do so, the traditional required curriculum will be dramatically transformed.

If curricular restructuring is to succeed, it appears that teachers will provide the leadership to rethink the content and structure of the traditional disciplines. Advances in information technologies now make it possible for teachers to be curriculum developers in ways that would have been a dream only 20 years ago. Restructuring may be achieved by literally thousands of teachers who rethink and reconfigure the curriculum through thousands of school-based curriculum development projects. The challenge will be to allow and encourage teachers to examine their content and to rethink how they teach their subjects, then support them as they develop and implement new curricula.

The dimension of curriculum is important for obvious reasons. However, much talk of restructuring shies away from this topic because the curriculum is so central to teachers' identities. Many "restructuring" projects consider changing everything other than curriculum. Changing what they teach is among the most difficult things for teachers to do. Therefore, to discuss changes in curriculum can be very threatening. Such discussions, however painful, are necessary. Next to curriculum, the area most difficult for teachers to change is instructional technique, which is considered next.

Instruction

One theme captures many of the emerging changes in instructional methods. It is that learners must be more actively engaged in learning. Examples of this trend abound. They range from whole language instruction in elementary schools to cooperative learning in secondary schools, community service in high schools, experience-based programs, and project-centered education at all levels. Philosophically, these forms of learning are based on the assumption that learners can and must make decisions about what they learn, and they must process and interpret what they learn to make it meaningful.

It is important to note that this notion of learning does not imply that students will learn less content, or that they will simply play at learning, retaining whatever they might glean from an activity. The goal is not simply to make learning enjoyable, although that can be a frequent positive side effect. The goal is to cause students to learn and retain significantly more information. Few programs of instruction are successful if students do not have some opportunity to add their own meaning to the material. If the movement toward high-content curricula described previously is to succeed, it will need to be linked with instructional techniques that foster the integration and retention of more content by students.

Examples of Some Instructional Practices That Engage Learners More Actively

There are many examples of techniques that engage learners more actively. Cooperative learning is one of the most prevalent and thoroughly tested. Its popularity has soared during the past decade. It has had to overcome concerns that it would undermine traditional American values of competition, that individual students would not be accountable for their own learning, and that high-achieving students would be dragged down or held back by the group. Cooperative learning practiced by properly trained teachers has been proven to address these concerns.

Cooperative learning is an example of a teaching strategy that results in solid achievement gains and improved social behavior with groups of students who have a wide range of abilities. Traditional teaching techniques aim at the mythical "middle" of the class and thereby ignore the needs of any student not in this category. Cooperative learning can meet the needs of all students. If schools want all students to succeed, a technique such as cooperative learning can be a powerful tool.

For teachers to incorporate cooperative learning successfully, they must be trained in its use, and they must also believe that all students can learn. Many teachers confuse group work with cooperative learning. Having students work in a group is not the same as a structured cooperative learning activity. Parents worry that cooperative learning means group grades. Once again, this is not the case, and those trained in its use understand how to employ cooperative learning so that students are held individually accountable for their learning even as they participate as part of a group.

The power of cooperative learning is that it puts learners at the center of the learning process and insists that they participate. Often, they must be given guidance on how to do so, but the journey is one toward learner independence, not dependence. Properly constructed assignments cause students to come to grips with material at a personal level—to incorporate it and retain it.

Whole-language approaches to literacy development are another way in which learners become more actively engaged in learning. In short, whole language means immersing the child in literacy, letting children see the possibilities and structures of literacy from a young age, and encouraging students to explore roles such as author, editor, and critic to see the uses and power of literacy. Whole-language is not the same as "look-say" or "whole word" methods of reading instruction. The organizing principle of whole-language instruction is individual interpretation and meaning-making by the learner. The teacher creates environments and experiences that allow learners to make choices about what they read, construct meaning from the materials they read, create written products, and extend understanding of written material, individually and with others. This method can be contrasted to approaches to reading instruction, such as basal reader series, that control nearly every aspect of the reading experience for students.

Many other instructional techniques allow the learner to be more actively engaged. Examples of these techniques include the following:

- Personal goal setting, where learning is based on the goals of the learner and where the learner relates the learning to personal interests
- Simulations and role plays, which, by their very nature, engage students actively and cause them to interpret and construct meaning
- Project-centered learning, where students develop products and projects that span several subjects and perhaps several weeks as well, a technique that has been popular with gifted and talented students for some time (for example, science fairs and programs such as Odyssey of the Mind)
- Peer tutoring and peer learning, where older students teach younger children, or where more advanced students help their peers

- Field-based learning, which involves the learner in settings outside the classroom
- Case-study approaches, where a real-world problem creates the framework for investigation inside and outside the classroom

These techniques all demand student involvement and engagement in learning at a much higher level than do the techniques used today in most American classrooms. Such approaches appear particularly promising with at-risk youth when combined with well-designed and well-implemented direct-instruction programs that provide for structured acquisition of key foundational skills that such learners need before they can take control of their learning effectively.

It is difficult to adopt new instructional methods. More is required than merely training teachers, although this alone is a significant challenge. The true "restructuring" of teaching and learning comes when teachers reshape their entire way of thinking about teaching and their role as teacher. Will teachers come to accept the idea that it is all right for all students to make choices about what they learn? Can teachers acknowledge that students actually control the learning process in a fundamental sense, and that the teacher's most promising role is that of facilitator, coach, diagnostician, and curriculum developer? These are profound shifts in the worldview of people whose worldviews are not often challenged. To incorporate such ideas and approaches requires not just training for teachers in new methods, but a restructuring of basic assumptions about learning and learners.

DISCUSSION QUESTIONS

1. How is curriculum selected, reviewed, and updated at the school?
2. What is the current state of the curriculum? Are all subjects current and up-to-date?
3. How does the curriculum balance depth with coverage?
4. In what ways does the curriculum integrate knowledge across subject areas? How fragmented or integrated does the curriculum appear from the student's perspective?
5. In what ways does the curriculum allow students to apply what they are learning?
6. How does instruction at the school engage students actively?
7. Are there any indications that students are not engaging actively in learning? Are there indications that they are?

6 *Changes Surrounding the Classroom*

The areas of curriculum, instruction, assessment, and standards discussed so far are at the heart of schooling. For that reason, they are very difficult to change. Many schools begin restructuring one step removed from these core areas and focus on changing the ways in which students are organized to learn. These changes include rethinking how students are grouped, how high schools are organized, how time is structured, how learning is moved beyond the school into the community, and how technology can be employed as a learning tool.

Changes in the Ways in Which Students Are Grouped for Learning

A multitude of projects and experiments seek to change the ways in which students are grouped for learning. Many elementary schools are experimenting with mixed-age, or multiage, groupings of various types, and having students stay with the same teacher for more than one year. They are working to have students from programs like Title 1 (Chapter 1) reading or special education remain in the regular classroom rather than be removed as they are currently. Secondary programs are experimenting with schools-within-schools, community-based education, and the elimination of grouping by ability into "tracks." Brief descriptions of these approaches follow.

Mixed-Age, or Multiage, Grouping

There is a great deal of experimentation occurring with mixed-age learning environments in elementary schools, particularly at the primary (grades K through 3) level. This approach, often called nongraded primary, is based on the premise that it is not useful to group children for instruction based solely on age. Instead, the key organizer should be the child's readiness to learn. Readiness is a combination of the child's developmental level, ability, motivation, and other factors, including chronological age. In multiage environments, children are grouped and regrouped to create a match between the task and the child. The curriculum is designed to offer experiences and activities that are appropriate to the child's developmental level.

Multiage grouping is not new. This technique has been popular at different times during the past 100 years. In fact, the one-room schoolhouse is the ultimate multiage program. Interest in this method is being triggered by the realization that the current age-based grouping model is convenient for the school, but doesn't necessarily meet the needs of many children. It is easier to organize students by age, but they may be less likely to learn.

Multiage grouping acknowledges the reality of child development, that different children grow and mature at different rates, particularly in their early years. Multiage grouping does not necessarily mean all the "slow" children are "held back" with younger children. In fact, in a multiage school, even those students who would be retained at grade level in other schools would find many more opportunities to interact with children their own age. Instead, this model requires frequent grouping and regrouping of students so that they are with others at a comparable developmental level for certain tasks, but with the group for other tasks that are not based on development.

For example, a student might be in a reading group with students spanning several years in age, participate with students of similar age as a team working on a project, enjoy physical activities with children of similar motor development, and participate in whole-group discussions with age mates. The key to making this method work is the grouping and regrouping of children based on criteria tied to student development and knowledge, not just age. To do this, teachers must be expert in child development and very knowledgeable about each child's capabilities. Once again, performance standards help teachers gauge how each child is progressing.

Creating Communities Within Schools

Large high schools and middle schools are experimenting with schools-within-schools to capture the advantages of both large and small schools in one physical location, to allow students to feel that they are part of a community of learners, and to expand the range of educational programs within the school. Teachers can work together to create smaller programs that reflect unique interests or focal points. Such settings create many more opportunities for students to feel part of something, to create stronger communities within schools. They can offer parents a way to have some choice regarding what type of program their child attends within the public schools. Evidence strongly suggests that students perform better in settings where they are known and cannot be anonymous, and where they are actively involved in activities. Schools-within-schools can provide such opportunities.

One of the dangers of schools-within-schools is that they often become dumping grounds for the unwanted, the difficult-to-teach, or the "at-risk" students (and for the nonconformist teachers). Although these students certainly need educational environments where their needs are addressed, there is little to suggest that these students benefit by concentrating them in one location. There is also little reason to think that schools-within-schools cannot meet the needs of all students. Many magnet programs in urban areas, for example, illustrate how specialized, focused programs can have broad appeal.

At the other end of the spectrum are schools-within-schools that become elite programs. They also can become places where one group of students segregates itself from the rest of the student population, but for different reasons. Experience suggests that when a school-within-a-school gains a reputation for being "better" than the rest of the school, there is pressure to disband it because of the subtle (or not-so-subtle) competition for students and the social ranking that begins to occur. These programs can threaten the rest of the school. Rather than eliminating successful programs, the rest of the school might learn from their successes. The culture of the school would have to support continuous improvement and new norms that expected teachers to learn from one another.

The premise behind all schemes for breaking down large, complex organizations into smaller subunits is that smaller structures will allow more opportunities for human interaction and affiliation to occur. In other words, the potential for stronger personal relationships to develop is enhanced. This sense of belonging and being valued appears to help learning occur, particularly for at-risk students. Small rural schools have proved this principle for years. Students center their lives on the school because that is the norm in their community. Within the school, most students develop a personal relationship with at least one teacher. When teachers know and understand a student, they do a better job of watching out for potential problems.

Rethinking Strategies for Grouping Students

Many schools are rethinking how students are grouped for instruction. The current grouping strategy that is being questioned most often is tracking—the practice of putting students into groups for long periods of time based on some measure of ability. Tracking tailors the curriculum and instruction to each group based on assumptions about what the students in the track are capable of learning. Students are retained in such groups over long periods and for a variety of subjects.

Sometimes the effect of grouping students even for only two or three subjects is to segregate them throughout the rest of the day as well. The choices open to them for the remainder of their schedule often dictate that they travel together throughout the day, even in classes where there is no rationale for grouping by ability. The net effect is that these students learn from one another, socialize with one another, come to define their abilities primarily in relation to one another, and take their cues for appropriate behavior from one another.

Clearly, this benefits some students significantly more than others. One of the other problems with tracking is that students in different tracks do not necessarily learn the same curriculum; they generally learn completely different curricula. Some are exposed to challenging concepts and interesting problems and assignments; others deal only with low-level factual material presented in the least interesting ways imaginable. Low-ability tracks come to focus on moving students through the system, and become less concerned with what the students are actually learning.

Alternatives to tracking are being pursued in some schools primarily to increase the educational success of all students. New practices are not being instituted simply to make students feel better about themselves nor strictly to benefit low-achieving students. The approaches being put into place are designed, for the most part, with the goal of providing richer educational experiences for all students and bringing techniques formerly reserved for talented and gifted students to all students.

When a school moves away from tracking, there is a ripple effect that travels throughout the school's instructional program. Successful alternatives to tracking seek to create a core curriculum rich in complex ideas and opportunities that all students must master. To accomplish this, teachers need a new curriculum that is designed to appeal and be accessible to a wide range of ability levels. Teachers also need an expanded repertoire of instructional methods. Additionally, some special needs students will require special support and accommodation, but still will be given as much of the same core curriculum as is feasible. At the same time, alternative assessment and grading practices have to be developed that allow a wider range of students to show what they have learned. Various support structures, such as tutoring and help centers, need to be available as well if all students are to learn roughly the same core material.

Including Special Education Students in the Regular Classroom

The attempt to decrease tracking and include all students in common, challenging learning experiences has led some schools to include special education students in regular education classrooms to the maximum extent possible. This trend represents a major challenge to most teachers and schools. Although efforts are under way to develop models such as consultative teachers and joint planning teams, a tremendous amount of work remains to be done before American classrooms can hope to accommodate wide ranges of student ability successfully.

The pressure for inclusion comes in part from democratic principles of equal treatment for all students and in part from the limited success that special education students have had in pullout programs. This is particularly true of learning-disabled students. This movement applies to all pullout programs, including Title 1 and other remedial approaches that remove the student from the regular classroom.

However, to include all students in the same classroom requires fundamental reorganization of curriculum, instruction, and assessment, as well as redeployment of resources, including professional staff, reconfiguration of time, integrated use of technology, and redefined parental involvement. The discussions of mainstreaming and full inclusion serve to highlight the challenges that the educational system faces in its attempt to meet the needs of all students to function at high levels cognitively and socially.

Integrating special needs students into classrooms represents a unique challenge to educators because these students represent two distinctly different groups of children. One group is composed of those who historically have not been included in public school classrooms with any regularity; among these are students with severe and profound physical and mental disabilities. Until federal legislation in the mid-1970s, these children were in special schools or programs devoted to and organized around their conditions. Regular classroom teachers often have little experience or training to prepare them to teach such students. These students are new, challenging, and sometimes just a bit frightening to veteran teachers.

The other group of special education students is those who were only recently withdrawn from regular education. These include children with learning disabilities and those who are emotionally or behaviorally disturbed. Such students were a part of regular education until the mid-1970s and the passage of federal special education legislation. Since that time, numerous special programs have been developed for such students, and many regular classroom teachers have ceased to accept responsibility for the instruction of these children.

To be successful, the integration of special education students will require a change in the culture of schools. Inclusion of these students implies that teachers will be responsible for the education of all students. Such a transformation will be exceedingly difficult to achieve in environments where teachers work in isolation from one another, set different standards of success, and hold differing expectations for appropriate student behavior. Also contributing to the complexity of change will be parent groups that support the rights of special needs students. These groups are well-organized and influential. Some are viewing the movement toward greater inclusion with a cautious eye because they fear losing the hard-won rights and special education services they have gained over the past 20 years.

Moving Learning Beyond the School

Another way in which the learning environment is being redefined is by moving more instruction outside classroom walls. One strategy being implemented in several states is the community service requirement, in which all students spend some time outside school working in volunteer positions to improve the community. Care must be taken when developing such a requirement not to make excessive or unreasonable demands on students' time. Many options should be available so that students can choose an option that interests them. At the same time, the general requirement can help students make connections between their learning and their community, as well as help them develop and mature.

When schools develop schedules that allot larger amounts of uninterrupted time to instruction, students can move outside of school for various learning activities. Examples include the following:

- More field work in science, social studies, math, and other classes
- More research projects that require sole-source documents, photographs, interviews, or other sources of data outside the school
- Assignments that require students to observe government, the courts, or other civic institutions in action
- Opportunities to observe and participate in the world of work

In communities with civic resources, schools have moved instruction into museums, arts centers, historical settings, and other locations that are rich in potential learning experiences for children but that are seldom used beyond the occasional visit.

New Kinds of Schools

There are many new approaches to schooling that break with traditional models. These include charter schools and various attempts to establish "break the mold" schools.

Charter Schools

Charter schools have gained the most attention recently because states have allowed limited numbers to be established. In brief, a charter school is a public school that operates directly on a charter from the state or the local board of education. It is both a part of and separate from the existing system and is not subject to the rules, regulations, and procedures of the school district in which it is located. Some charters remain affiliated with a school district, whereas others report directly to a state board of education.

The conditions under which charters can be granted differ from state to state. Some stipulate that certified teachers continue to be employed. Others require the consent of the local teachers' union or of teachers in any building that is to convert to a charter. Most states demand evidence that the charters result in improved student performance in relation to agreed-upon standards for the charter to be renewed.

The idea behind charter schools is that by freeing schools from the bonds and boundaries of bureaucracy, they can adapt to the needs of students. Charter schools cannot open or remain in business without voluntary participation by students. They must "sell" themselves and appeal to a segment of the population if they are to survive. They must also demonstrate success with students. In theory, they can explore new ways of teaching and learning and can provide a type of controlled competition to the existing system, encouraging it to adapt and incorporate the best techniques from the charters into every school.

In practice, charter schools have proven to be more complicated and have not always achieved their aims. It can be much easier to imagine a school than to run one, a lesson that idealistic teachers, parents, or community members have learned the hard way. It is also very difficult to do education in substantially different ways than it is being done currently. Most people went to school with the same basic model of learning. They carry it with them and tend to reinvent it, even if they do so unconsciously.

Furthermore, some special interest groups have seized upon charter schools as vehicles to establish what amounts to public private schools. By creating a focus, philosophy, or set of requirements unlikely to appeal to most parents, they ensure that the school will be populated primarily by those with similar belief systems. There are certainly reasons for people with similar beliefs to band together to educate their children. However, in the postsegregation era, public schools have been theoretically open to everyone, and some charter schools appear to be moving outside of this ideal, at least in spirit.

At the same time, charters have been demonstrating innovative approaches to teaching and learning. Most require more parental involvement than traditional schools. Many are more fully integrated into the community. Some put technology much more at the center of learning. Most of the successful ones are staffed by excited, innovative teachers who finally have the opportunity to put their ideas into practice. Charters continue to hold great promise as one more way that schools can learn new techniques and structures to incorporate into the larger system of public education.

"Break the Mold" Schools

There have been several notable attempts to redesign schools "from the ground up." Several of these have been sponsored by private foundations like the New American Schools Development Corporation. All of these efforts have encountered similar difficulties in trying to "reinvent" education. They experience some of the same challenges faced by charter school advocates; rarely do you ever begin with a blank sheet of paper when redesigning education.

At the same time, these various experiments continue to test new techniques and structures. They involve the community to a greater degree. Virtually all of these new models try to improve school readiness. They seek new relationships between community and school. They increase the use of technology, integrate it more, and make it central to instruction. They alter school schedules and calendars; increase participation in decisions; use a wide variety of new ways to assess student knowledge; redefine teachers as guides and coaches; integrate the curriculum; and attempt to use the results from the best research on effective teaching, learning, and school structure.

So they are different; yet in some ways they are the same in their differentness. They are important because educators are cautious and will look to new models first before moving too far from the proven track. So it is perhaps not surprising that even the "break the mold" schools generally dent the mold more than break it. If they differed too much from today's schools, they would be hard pressed to find many parents who would allow their children to attend. At the same time, they run the risk of quickly reverting to rather traditional-looking school programs if they cannot define themselves as fundamentally different from today's schools. It will be informative to watch their progress and development over time.

Changing the Structure of Time

Many educators and students are frustrated with the way time is structured in schools. Learning is broken into many fragmented pieces, generally too short to allow serious and thoughtful engagement with the content being taught. School schedules allot roughly the same amount of time to each learning task, regardless of the real needs of the topic or material being taught. The urge to redefine time limits is often particularly strong in high schools, where the six, seven, or eight-period day arbitrarily divides learning into many chunks, almost always less than an hour each. However, elementary schools also break the day into many small units of teaching time, some as small as 20 minutes.

One example of an innovative model for reconfiguring time is the Copernican Plan. Designed for use at the high school level, this plan centers around the idea of "macroclasses" of differing possible lengths, from 70 to 226 minutes. It emphasizes the integration of subject matter through seminars. The curriculum becomes less fragmented because students take fewer courses at any given time. Teachers teach fewer classes each day, thereby reducing the number of students they see each day. One goal is to improve students' sense of belonging and to increase teachers' ability to meet students' individual needs. These benefits in turn can lead to greater student success and increased motivation.

Another strategy is block scheduling. In general, block schedules double or triple the amount of time each course meets by reducing the number of periods in the day and increasing the length of each. There are many variations on this model. In most, year-long courses are taught in a semester. In this fashion, students can accumulate as least as many credits in a year as they do under conventional schedules. If students take four classes a day for two semesters in a block schedule, they earn the same credit as if they take eight year-long classes in a typical semester system. The advantages to teachers are that they teach only three courses (and have one planning period) per semester; they see fewer students each day because they are teaching three classes, not five; and their preparation period always borders an additional block of time (before school, lunch, after school). Teachers also end up teaching six classes in a year rather than five, allowing more choices for students.

Although a semester course meets fewer minutes than its year-long equivalent under the block, teachers report that they are able to teach comparable amounts of material. Additional time is gained by decreasing the number of transitions and housekeeping tasks required to pass between each class. The time available can be used more effectively. Student involvement and attention can be enhanced because students spend more time on learning tasks. Teachers who work in schools with block schedules report that they have more time to provide attention to individual students and to adapt lessons to the needs of each class. In addition, administrators and teachers report that students seem less stressed and more able to focus. Students seem to agree with this assessment.

Block schedules also allow and sometimes prod teachers to employ a wider array of instructional strategies. However, this does not occur in every instance. In some cases, teachers simply teach two lessons per period. Or, teachers use the extra time to allow students to do the lesson's homework in class. Other problems result when students are not scheduled into a class for 90 minutes at a time, and there is little to occupy them at the school during their free time. Many parents of children who are college-bound worry that it will be more difficult for their children to do well on tests like Advanced Placement, PSAT, and SAT if much time elapses between when material is taught and when these tests are given.

None of these problems is insoluble. Schools have developed solutions to all these issues, but only through careful and thoughtful planning. In particular, teachers need to be involved in designing the specific schedule to be used because there is no one right model. Many possibilities exist. Furthermore, time and resources must be available to assist teachers in adapting their curriculum and teaching techniques to the potentialities and challenges of the new schedule.

Middle schools, in particular, are implementing approaches that have groups of teachers and students staying together for more than one period. In such a model, 100 students might each have the same four teachers for Periods 1 through 4 for the same subjects (for example, language arts, science, social studies, art). This averages out to 25 students per teacher per period in this example. Assuming 45-minute periods, the four teachers would have three hours total to structure however they saw fit because the students would not report to any other teachers during that time. They could choose to keep students in groups of 25 per teacher and vary the time they spent in each class, or they could meet with larger or smaller groups of students each day. In other words, some days one teacher might take most of the students for some activity while the other three were free to work with small groups or individual students for an extended time.

Although multiperiod blocks are by no means new, they can be a valuable tool to enable faculties to achieve a number of goals simultaneously. Common planning time can be created for teachers who work together in blocks. Teachers can discuss the problems and needs of individual students because they are likely to know each student. Such environments can be much more supportive to students with disabilities and can accommodate supported education, where a special education teacher is in the classroom to assist mainstreamed students. Other specialists, including a counselor or reading specialist, can be "assigned" to a block. Their services are provided in the context of the block. They become part of the block "community." Students can be pulled out periodically without disrupting their learning or schedule nearly as much.

The potential of block scheduling still may be difficult to realize. Teachers may not want larger blocks of time because they do not have the time (or inclination) to redesign their curriculum and instruction accordingly, or they lack the desire to work with a team of teachers. Most teachers do not have professional experiences that prepare them to plan collaboratively or to work closely with colleagues, which a block schedule arrangement requires.

Technology as a Learning Tool

The most striking observation one reaches about the role of technology in education over the past 12 years is not its impact but its lack of impact. The places where technology has had an impact most often are the central offices of midsized or larger school districts, and in school offices where staff must manage data on student schedules, attendance, and transcripts. But technology has not revolutionized learning in the classroom, nor has it yet led to increased productivity in schools.

The only technologies that have firmly taken root in most schools are the copier (which simply replaced the ditto machine) and the videotape recorder and television monitor (which replaced the 16mm projector and screen). In the vast majority of schools, telephones are still not readily available to teachers. Voice mail systems (not answering machines) are just beginning to be seen in some schools. Fax machines are a part of most central offices but are just now appearing in school buildings. Many schools either cannot afford the cost of an additional phone line, or their equipment is so antiquated that the entire system has to be replaced to accommodate something as simple as a fax. In many districts, these forms of telecommunication are not even included in the district's overall plan for technology because parents, teachers, and community members usually associate technology with only one thing: the computer. They overlook many other important and ubiquitous forms of technology.

Some Often-Overlooked Technologies

Telephones, fax machines, and video cameras are less glamorous than computers, and for that reason their potential benefits for instruction often go unnoticed. While schools flock to install satellite dishes, computer networks, or elaborate Integrated Learning Systems (a computer lab with structured software in a particular subject or subjects), the most basic form of telecommunication, the telephone, often remains overlooked as a potential tool, both for teacher productivity and student learning. Telephone lines possess the ability to carry voice, electronic, and visual data. The telephone can serve as a tool for better communication between teachers and parents. If phones are available, teachers will use them. If they are inconvenient to use, teachers will be much less inclined to make repeated efforts to reach parents, for example.

Phone lines also allow students to communicate with others in the local community and around the world. Conference calls allow direct, real-time communication; computer networks, such as National Geographic's Kidnet, allow electronic communication. On-line databases also can be accessed through conventional phone lines, putting vast amounts of information at the fingertips of teachers and students. Recent developments in video transmission technologies are allowing phone lines to transmit video images to accompany a conversation. And the Internet, which will be discussed later, is a potential gateway to information of nearly unlimited variation and source.

Access to a telephone line also creates the capability of employing a fax machine in a variety of ways. This simple technology has the advantage of requiring almost no training, yet it can be used almost as effectively as a computer for quick communication over distances. The fax can even be used to communicate with parents, many of whom now have access to a fax (or have one in their own home).

The video camera, a powerful, accessible tool for curriculum development and student expression, is viewed more as a toy than an educational tool. It is ironic that video is largely ignored at the same time that students spend large blocks of their leisure time viewing information from video sources. Visual images are an increasingly important part of students' lives, and of most workplaces, yet video clearly remains on the fringes of instruction in schools. Low-cost editing equipment and small, portable cameras with relatively sophisticated technical features enable children and adults to collect and organize visual information with relative ease. Advances in multimedia technologies are leading to the integration of video and computer-based information.

Distance Learning

Telecommunication in the form of satellite transmissions, generally referred to as distance learning, is being employed by more and more schools throughout the country. This combination is especially appealing to rural schools as a source of learning experiences that they are otherwise unable to offer. Interactive distance learning also offers a way for students to communicate with other children in very different environments, thereby counteracting the sense of isolation often present in rural settings. Although distance learning may prove to be a powerful tool for restructuring, its use at this point is primarily to expand, not to change, the existing curriculum by offering courses such as physics or French to schools not otherwise able to offer them.

As educators become more familiar and comfortable with the potential inherent in distance learning, and as more schools purchase the equipment necessary to participate fully in satellite uplink-downlink, it is likely that these technologies will be employed to restructure as well as expand the curriculum. If nothing else, telecommunication allows rural schools to adapt rapidly (sometimes more rapidly than their larger urban cousins). For example, rural schools with interactive capacity are offering courses in foreign languages such as Japanese and Chinese. These courses are taught by highly trained teachers, often native speakers, whereas urban schools, relying on their own teachers, may have to limit their offerings to the "traditional" European languages.

Emerging Multimedia and Network Technologies

One other promising area of rapidly emerging technologies is multi-media. Multimedia combines computer, video, audio, and other sources, such as on-line data, in a way that allows users to interact with information and make decisions about how and what they learn. Like many recent technologies, multimedia has received considerable hype as the next tool to revolutionize education and schooling.

Multimedia gives students the opportunity not only to research the written word, but to employ graphic images and full-motion video in combination with text to create an integrated report. Students become much more involved in the decision-making process concerning both what they learn and how they organize and present what they have learned.

Local Area Networks (LANs) provide the potential to link learners and teachers within a school. This technology is becoming very common in the workplace, where work teams are simultaneously contributing to a product or document that exists only on the network until it is finally printed out. Learning in schools could be transformed if learners were linked. Students would not have to meet physically or leave class to work on projects. Students could be grouped without modifying their schedules. LANs also provide the capability for teachers to work collaboratively and to share as well. Additionally, both students and teachers can call in from home to the LAN and continue their work outside of school hours.

The Internet and Networking

The Internet is truly a phenomenon. It has burst upon the scene and continues to grow and evolve rapidly and unpredictably. What the Internet does demonstrate conclusively is the capability to create complex networks of computers exchanging a wide range of information and the willingness and enthusiasm of people to learn how to use this network.

The Internet has two possible primary uses for schools: as a research tool and as a communication tool. As a research tool, it offers access to an unimaginably large amount of data from an incredible array of sources. It is easy to search and reasonably fun to use, particularly when compared to older command-line interfaces that are dependent on obscure written commands. As a communication tool, it can allow students to converse with experts and novices on any of a wide range of topics. Through bulletin boards and file transfer programs, students can quickly obtain advice and assistance from around the world. These communications can be interesting, entertaining, and informative. Students are drawn into the world of the Internet. Sometimes, the challenge is to get them to rejoin the world outside of it.

In the long run, the Internet poses a unique challenge that goes far beyond these two uses. If virtually everyone has access to the Internet, if it continues to become easier to use, if the range of things that can be done on it continues to grow, and if schools don't become dramatically more technology rich, we may be faced with a situation in which children are exposed to so much information in the home and elsewhere in their lives that school becomes the place they go to get away from data and information.

This may seem preposterous on the surface, and may be. However, it is worth asking the question now because educators are not likely to hold the monopoly on knowledge they have had previously. Home schooling, in particular, has gained momentum using rather unimaginative packaged curriculum programs. It is worth pondering how many more families may choose some degree of home schooling if they can gain easy access to relatively inexpensive, high-quality learning materials coupled with teacher interaction electronically over the Internet.

The Internet need not be the kind of threat to schools that it (or some other variation, such as enhanced cable television) is likely to be to the postal service. At the same time, the handwriting is on the wall for all to see. Simply outfitting schools with computers does not give them any particular advantage over the home or any other site that would choose to establish an electronic hookup. The difference, or "value added," that schools can offer is in how they structure, support, facilitate, and certify student learning. But for schools to contribute some unique "value added" in this area, technology cannot continue to be marginalized the way it is currently, nor can it be optional, nor can schools wait until there is "enough money" before they purchase technology. Many teachers and administrators respond with the lament, "But we can't afford to," when they might more fruitfully determine if they can afford not to.

DISCUSSION QUESTIONS

1. What is the balance between "order and warmth" in the school?
2. How do the ways in which students are grouped reflect values and beliefs in the school?
3. How is the school's instructional program organized to accommodate the many challenges that students bring to school, including learning and behavioral problems?
4. How successful are students who participate in pull-out or other special programs? At what point do they rejoin the mainstream?
5. How does the school take advantage of the community to enrich learning opportunities?
6. What would be the effect if students and parents were able to make some choices about where and how schooling took place?
7. To what degree are teachers and students able to adapt time to the needs of learning, rather than adapting learning to the needs of time?
8. How would you assess the role of technology in the school? Is it integral? Are adults proficient in technology? Do students have easy access to technology? Are the technologies current?
9. What might be the effects of upgrading basic technologies, such as telephones, in the school?
10. In what ways is the school a gateway to information? In what ways is it a bottleneck?
11. What is the school's or district's plan for integrating and updating technology?

PART III

How Will Roles Change for Educators and Community Members?

7 *Changing Roles of Educators and Students*

When schools change, the roles of the adults and children in schools change, too. Roles are the social behaviors expected of an individual in any given setting. Right now, everyone in a school knows his or her role. Role changes are difficult, particularly for adults who have acted a particular way their entire careers. Even students find it difficult when they are expected to act differently. This chapter explores the ways in which the roles of principal, teacher, and student may change when schools are restructured.

The Changing Role of the Principal

In schools where considerable effort has been devoted to restructuring, the role of the principal is often very different from the historically familiar role of a strong, forceful leader. Principals in schools that are restructuring demonstrate a broader range of skills. They lead not by dictating but by facilitating. They are still respected leaders who can make difficult decisions, but they do not make those decisions in isolation from the staff. Instead, they work in what might be best described as a partnership with staff, each having responsibilities and each bringing certain skills to the relationship. Some behaviors that principals bring to this partnership include the following.

Having a Clear Sense of Purpose Linked to a Vision for the School. Principals' actions and decisions are guided by a vision of education. When principals talk of a vision, they mean an overall sense of where the school is headed, the goals off in the distance toward which the school should be striving. Vision may reside in the principal as an individual, but more frequently, it is created jointly with the staff. Sometimes, the principal blends in his or her personal vision with the school's, influencing but not dominating it.

All important decisions are linked to the vision. It serves as a screen through which new ideas, proposals, and programs are viewed and evaluated. The principal is the bridge between the vision and the specific programs undertaken to make the vision a reality.

Using Information From Many Sources to Create the Vision and Make Decisions. The principal helps to ensure that information is used to support development and implementation of the vision. Information comes from many sources, including student achievement, discipline, and attendance; surveys of parents and students; and follow-up studies of graduates, dropouts, and others who have left the school. Other sources include reports on the latest educational and societal trends, as well as ideas or findings from journals, books, conferences, professional meetings, and visitations to other schools or sites. The principal helps others to obtain and organize this information.

Principals frequently take the responsibility of keeping up-to-date on new developments in a range of areas related to the vision. They attend conferences, read voraciously, discuss ideas with colleagues, copy articles, and distribute them to the faculty. They encourage faculty to examine their current practices and to consider new approaches and ideas.

Information about current practices and new approaches provides a basis for discussions of possible school goals. Using data and ideas has the effect of helping to neutralize some of the opposition to or fear of change present in every school. The use of information also moves the principal out of a controlling role, thereby deflecting suspicions that the process is being manipulated to serve the principal's agenda. Data, to a certain degree, speak for themselves.

Teachers have difficulty being involved in decision making in any meaningful way if they do not have the information necessary to make good decisions. Principals provide information to teachers to enable them to make decisions about budget, staffing, building schedules, and the instructional program.

Principals also provide information about how the school functions internally, how money is allocated, what resources are available, and how operational decisions are made. By moving these issues into the public light, suspicion is decreased. At the same time, the quality of decisions made by teachers is enhanced when they can see the impact of their decisions on other aspects of the school or can suggest solutions to the real problems they see in the school.

Allocating Resources Consistent With the Vision. Having developed and agreed upon a common focus or purpose as expressed in a vision, principals facilitate the vision by allocating resources in a way that moves the school toward its goals. For example, the school budget may be developed jointly with teachers as a tool to achieve the vision, or space may be reallocated to create specific activities or programs. This replaces what is commonly called the "squeaky wheel" method of management, where the most strident or unpleasant people get what they want, or the equally undesirable "paternalistic" method, where the principal doles out resources to teachers as if they were children.

Creating New Ways to Make Decisions. As facilitators, principals have to work with existing decision-making methods, recognizing their limitations. Many of these methods were designed to maintain the school's current practices, not to adapt or improve them. Rather than redesign these methods, what many principals have chosen to do is to create entirely new ways to make decisions. They involve people in different ways and allow new leaders to emerge. Principals are not necessarily "in control" of these methods. In other words, having created a new leadership structure, the principal then stands back and lets people make decisions and, in the process, relinquishes a significant amount of personal control.

In the process of "letting go," principals learn how to support decision making from the sidelines. Sometimes, this requires them simply to remain silent in a meeting; other times, it means trusting teachers to make good decisions and allowing them to do so even if the decisions are not the same ones that the principal would make.

Letting go and supporting works best if the principal has many informal interactions with teachers in place of formal, one-way communication. The principal is constantly taking the pulse of the school. This process of letting go is not easy, even for those principals who are committed to changing. However, those who have done so report that they are much more effective than they were before because they are now working as the agent of the group, rather than singlehandedly attempting to change the school or being viewed as an adversary by many.

Challenges of Role Transition

The preceding section on the new role of the principal illustrates how principals facilitate rather than control change in their buildings. This new way of doing business can be fraught with difficulties, particularly for principals who were selected for their ability to be "strong leaders," which has been interpreted to mean being able to impose one's will on others. Essentially, these people are being asked to modify their personalities. To change one's personality dramatically is a tremendously difficult thing to expect of any adult, particularly of those who feel that they are currently doing a competent job and see little reason to change.

There is an additional challenge. Even as principals are involving more people in decision making, the principal alone continues to bear the brunt of responsibility for achieving school goals and improving student performance. Many principals justifiably worry about being held responsible for decisions they have not made. This new role for the principal has many unanswered questions and unresolved issues; however, it appears that the best way to improve schools is to involve those who do the work in determining how to make it work better. Schools cannot be improved beyond a certain point by simply dictating.

Changing the Role of Teacher

When restructuring is attempted with some success, there is a strong likelihood that the role of teacher will change at least as much as the principal. Schools that are restructuring generally tend to "professionalize" the role of teacher. This means that teachers make many more decisions and select the programs and methods they believe will work best for their students. They spend more time discussing the school's goals, vision, and purpose, as well as its effects on students.

If teachers are to have greater decision-making authority, they will have to interact successfully with one another more than they do currently, and will have to do so in a frank manner. They will need to be able to communicate, negotiate, seek consensus, set goals, and resolve conflict successfully. Teachers rarely develop these skills in schools where they operate in isolation.

However, in schools where teachers talk about effective practices and school goals, decisions made by teachers have effects on all teachers in the school. Making the change from teachers who expect to be left alone, and who expect decisions not to affect them, to teachers who are making decisions that affect the total school requires very different norms and values within the school and new skills by the teachers.

When restructuring causes teachers to develop new roles, teachers quickly gain a broader perspective on their role in the organization. As they begin to make more complex decisions, they come to grips with the implications of these decisions. They must deal with issues such as the effect of changing someone's teaching assignment, how contracts and laws limit their choices, an unanticipated reaction to a decision, or an unintended effect on their colleagues of a particular action. For many teachers, this broader view is new and somewhat uncomfortable. Decisions that seemed so simple when the principal made them suddenly become very complex. Some teachers lose their nerve at this point and want to return responsibility to the administrator.

Administrators have an important role to play in this process. They help teachers deal with situations that are beyond their control or that are particularly complex or conflict laden, but attempt to do so without taking total control. Once teachers make a difficult decision, the principal supports the decision by implementing it. Principals may organize the training that teachers need to develop necessary group-process and decision-making skills.

With greater authority comes greater accountability for teachers. One of the key principles of having teachers participate in decisions is that student learning will improve as a result. In the past, it was possible to blame the central office or principal when things went wrong. When decisions are made at the school by the teachers, it is more difficult to do so. Teachers may find themselves being asked to explain why student learning is not improving, or to demonstrate how a particular decision improves student learning.

Current attempts at site-based decision making rarely link decision-making authority and improved student learning. If this link is forged, teachers will look at their involvement in decision making differently. They will have become professionals in the truest sense of the word, setting the conditions of their work and accepting responsibility for the results.

The partnership between teacher and parent also changes as schools restructure. Many schools limit the role of parents today. Schools may want parents simply to do what they are asked to do, to support school activities, classroom discipline, and student homework assignments. Although parental support for teacher decisions is vitally important, there is more to this relationship than having parents do what teachers or principals ask them to do.

As a school restructures, the teacher's expectations for the parent are spelled out more clearly. In addition, the parent's expectations for the teacher are stated. The teacher also solicits information on the student's interests, personality, and other factors that might affect performance. The ritualistic parent-teacher conference may be replaced with more genuine interactions, perhaps in the home of the student, that lead to an exchange of perceptions and a greater understanding of the goals of each party. Parents, and students, have additional implied responsibilities that will be discussed in more detail.

Changing the Role of Student

To become actively engaged in learning, students need to have some control over what they learn. They need opportunities to make more decisions about their learning. They need to accept the consequences of their decisions. With responsibility comes accountability. One way to accomplish this is to have learners develop personal learner goals linked to performance standards. Students then report on their progress toward achieving these goals. They demonstrate publicly their efforts and accomplishments. This approach can create personal accountability in front of parents, peers, teachers, and community members. Students cannot remain anonymous. They cannot avoid taking any responsibility for their learning, as many do currently.

In addition, students need opportunities to collaborate, and to work together to solve real problems. To do so, students will need to exercise control over the pace of learning and the learning activities themselves. They will need to ask questions, study topics that they deem important, and construct and produce knowledge.

Students who are now drifting through school will need to be challenged to become much more aware of their personal strengths and weaknesses. They will have to accept, even demand, formative feedback so that they can assess their skills and knowledge more accurately against clear standards. They will need to be willing to set longer term goals, longer than "passing the test," and to think about how their choices for an education will affect them in the long run. They will start to think about the relationship between what they are doing in school and what they will be doing when they leave school. They will begin to think of how their behaviors help or hinder achievement of their life goals. Having made these linkages, they will have to be willing to work much harder to produce much higher quality work than they do currently. Their expectations for themselves and for the work they produce will need to rise, along with teachers' and parents' expectations for them.

College-bound students will be called upon to reexamine the cynical transactional relationship they frequently develop with teachers, counselors, and administrators, where every activity is judged on how it contributes to college admission. Students should be encouraged to attempt difficult and challenging learnings, to develop their minds and truly master material, not merely to generate high grade point averages.

They should be able to take courses that are challenging and that help them develop their intellect, even if there is risk of not getting an "A." They should have the chance to see and understand the world of work and its relationship to their lives. Thus, they should have the opportunity to participate in activities such as internships, apprenticeships, shadowing experiences, and other chances to understand the world they are entering; to see that cooperative teamwork is as important as individual achievement; to understand what quality work is; to be more aware of the need to think critically and solve problems; and to develop skills that make them successful, lifelong learners.

These types of skills are often identified as being important for success in the workplace of the future. College-bound students may inadvertently neglect the development of these skills if they overemphasize individual achievement. High-achieving students can be expected to do much more than they do currently, not in terms of quantity, but in terms of depth of understanding and application.

Furthermore, high school students must reassess the appropriateness of holding a job that has no relation to what they are learning and where they want to go with their lives. The jobs, often for minimum wage, offer little future for most students while detracting substantially from the time they have to devote to school. Students will have to weigh the relative benefits of near-full-time employment during high school. The school can help by providing more work experiences that can link to a student's program of study.

DISCUSSION QUESTIONS

1. How is the role of the principal in this school defined formally? How is it defined informally?

2. What is the history of leadership styles in the school? Have they been consistent or varied? What is the effect?

3. How do teachers view their role in the school? To what degree do they feel capable of changing the school so that they can be more successful with students?

4. How do students view their role in the school? What points of view exist? How much responsibility and ownership do they take for their own learning?

8 *Changing Roles of Parents and Community*

There is a growing realization that schools cannot educate children in isolation from the community and world in which the children live. Schools are no longer separate from the communities that surround them. Schools are contributing members of healthy communities, and are sometimes an oasis in neighborhoods where raising children can be difficult. For schools to be assets to their communities, and for the communities to support their children's education, the roles that parents, nonparents, community organizations, and businesses play change. In general, more is expected of people and organizations. Raising children successfully is an increasingly difficult task. It is one of the key reasons that school restructuring is necessary. The remainder of the chapter explores some of the ways that these roles are changing, beginning with parents.

The Role of Parents

More responsibility for educating the young in this country has been gradually transferred from the parent, the extended family, and the community at large to professional educators. Over the past 150 years, parents and communities have come to expect that if they pay their taxes, schools will educate the young. They are purchasing a service in much the same way that most large communities purchase fire, police, sanitation, and public welfare services. The expectation is that well-trained professionals will ensure that students are educated. This is called the "delegation model," meaning that responsibilities have been delegated to others who are paid to assume them.

There are limits to the delegation model. Communities cannot delegate too much responsibility for basic services unless the community is also supporting the professionals who provide the services. Police officers, for example, once relied on healthy neighborhoods to make sure that most residents obeyed the law or at least the rules of the neighborhood. With the breakdown of strong neighborhoods, local police departments have discovered the same thing that educators have: The safety of the community cannot be delegated to a few trained professionals who are not a part of the neighborhood or community.

Many rural communities acknowledge the need to work together for civic survival, often because there is no other alternative. Volunteer fire departments are only one example of how people participate actively to maintain their community. It is clear that participation and a strong sense of personal responsibility are essential to healthy communities.

Public education has gone in the opposite direction the past 50 years. When a principal or teacher contacts a parent regarding a problem that a child may be having, the parent may reply, "You're the educator. You're paid to educate. You deal with the problem." Educators get frustrated when they hear this, yet they may have inadvertently contributed to its development. The public schools have become insulated from the communities they serve. In many communities, and especially in urban areas, teachers tend to live outside the communities in which they teach. The principal and the central office serve as barriers and buffers between schools and parents. Laws and contracts specify many school operations and parent rights. Even school boards over time have come to protect professional educators from parents and community.

These buffers are absolutely necessary. If they did not exist, schools would quickly become politicized and fragmented. Schools do need some protection from individuals and groups who would manipulate education in harmful ways, some of whom are irritating, others of whom are downright dangerous. However, schools may have gone too far in insulating themselves, leading parents and community members to believe that they have little or no responsibility for education beyond paying taxes.

Because the schools have put in place many barriers to parental involvement, it appears that schools will have to begin the process of reconnecting with the community. Educators can foster communication with parents. They can involve them in setting educational and personal goals for their children. The school and home can jointly support student achievement.

There is ample evidence that student learning increases when parents are allowed to share the responsibility for educating their children. Parents who devote more time to all aspects of their children's education—not just helping them do homework—have children with more positive attitudes toward school and better achievement. In many places, parents are now invited to school to be entertained, lectured, or solicited for money. Schools need to provide many more opportunities and options for parents to participate in their child's education. Parents can

- Come to school to see their child demonstrate skills (not just perform)
- Assist in the development of student projects
- Receive briefings on the status of school goals and student performance in relation to goals
- Learn about the standards their child must meet
- Participate in learning activities with their child
- Assist in decision making and goal setting
- Help create a share sense of community centering on the school

These types of involvement can occur in the inner city as well as the suburbs if schools acknowledge the realities of the neighborhood as a starting point and proceed accordingly.

Here are some examples of how parents can become more involved in their child's education.

Becoming Knowledgeable About the Standards Their Children Are Expected to Meet. As schools develop clearer expectations for the things that a child must know and be able to do, parents need to be familiar with these expectations. They then will be more able to determine if their child is making adequate progress. They will have samples of acceptable student work to see how their child compares to peers. These samples are better than a letter grade because parents get a clearer idea of the quality of their child's work. This in turn suggests more clearly the ways in which parents can help the child improve to meet standards. When parents review student work or attend a demonstration by their child, they will see the level of student performance. They will know if their child is progressing at an acceptable rate, and they will know if their efforts are paying off in terms of better student performance.

Setting Learning Goals With the Teacher and Child. If students can set individualized learning goals, parents can help their child set appropriate goals and can monitor progress toward achievement of the goals. The teacher makes sure that the goals relate to district and state performance standards. Parents can then work with the child outside of school time to help the child achieve the goal, with the teacher providing guidance to the parent on the best way to assist.

Goals also create a common focus for parent-teacher conferences in which students report on their goal attainment. Grades and standardized achievement tests, by contrast, provide few specific things that students can do, except "read better," "spell better," or "learn your math facts."

Becoming Involved in Site-Based Decision Making. Parent involvement in decision making has tended to be carefully controlled by educators. When there is an opening on a committee or decision-making group, principals may slip into the role of Louis, the police chief in the movie *Casablanca,* who, whenever something went wrong, instructed his officers to "round up the usual suspects."

The parent from the PTA or the parent aide in the library contributes a great deal to schools. I do not want to denigrate their contributions. These individuals can be excellent representatives because they care and because they are knowledgeable about the school and committed to its success. However, these parents may not be as likely to challenge teacher and administrator views because in some ways they have become like staff members.

Schools should be open to a wide range of parental participation in site-based decision making, including parents who challenge the school's current practices and assumptions. Educators rarely seek such points of view, but divergent thinking can be very useful when attempting major school redesign. Educators together will have to be willing to take some chances by allowing new voices to enter the decision-making arena.

In many schools, there are new opportunities for parents to be involved in decision making. School site councils, in particular, provide a chance for parents to be heard and to influence the school's educational program. However, parent participation in such groups must be nurtured and encouraged. They must feel they are making a difference, having an impact, if they are to devote the time and energy necessary to make good decisions.

Advocating and Supporting Change in Schools. Most parents are not very aware of what is occurring in their child's classroom—the actual activities and curriculum being taught or skills being developed (beyond the basics). Even fewer could state the reasons why there is a need to change education. Many parents react to change in their child's school with anxiety and concern. They may have faith in their child's teacher, but little faith in the educational system, which they may view as being subject to fads and too willing to "experiment" on their child. Even worse, they may be disinterested entirely in the activities at the school.

Such attitudes can be overcome only by engaging parents to a greater degree in discussions about why change in education is necessary. This means, at a minimum, talking about the limits of the school's current program, without blaming anyone or suggesting that someone is doing a poor job. Educators are often reluctant to raise such issues because to do so implies that the school is doing something wrong. If parents are ever likely to advocate or at least support change, they will first need to be given the opportunity to become knowledgeable about the need for change.

For their part, parents will have to be more willing to make the connection between changes they can clearly see in the world at large, in the society, in their community, and in their workplace, and the implications that these changes have for schooling. They must be more willing to understand the degree to which education will have to change if it is to adapt to a rapidly changing world. Given the demands on parents' time currently, asking them to think about these issues intelligently is a difficult challenge for all involved.

Finding Time to Become Involved in Their Children's Education. As busy as most parents have become, the options that schools give them to be involved are nonoptions for many, who find it difficult just to keep up with work and home responsibilities. To deal with this problem, the school must begin to define reasonable expectations for involvement as well as a menu of realistic options. Parents then can be given support and assistance in choosing from among these. Those parents who choose not to participate can be contacted (preferably by other parents) to determine the reasons for not being involved. Suitable times or activities can then be arranged.

Videotape of special school events can allow parents to see how their children behave in school. Written material that outlines the expectations for parental involvement in assignments and projects throughout the year can be sent home for review early in the year. Parents can then anticipate upcoming projects and understand what they are expected to do. The specific skills necessary to assist on the project or task (along with necessary materials and equipment) can be explained and reviewed.

The home visit, once a fixture of most social service agencies and now nearly nonexistent, can be revived. Parents will need to know how and when to request a visit for noncrisis reasons. A home visit can and should be a time to foster genuine, two-way communication between school and home, to invite the parent to be involved in the child's education, and to celebrate something about the child.

These ideas require obvious, significant changes in the structure and organization of the school day and the teachers' contract because more interactions between teachers and parents might occur outside of school hours and off school grounds.

In essence, schools must come to expect more parental involvement. The school must take the lead in determining the nature of that involvement but should be less reticent about expecting it. Parents cannot be compelled to participate, but when an expectation is communicated consistently and reasonable accommodations are made, many more parents will feel willing (or obligated) to make the effort to become more involved with their children's education.

Education and parenting are two intertwined activities. Teachers and parents can support, but not replace, one another. Each must accept his or her responsibilities and the need to work together for the benefit of the child. Parental apathy is the norm in many schools. It cannot continue unchallenged. Educators are the ones who will need to take the lead by redefining this relationship, but parents will be called upon to rethink their expectations and assumptions for public education as well. This is a dialogue that, if successful, will spread beyond teachers and parents to include the broader community.

If schools make it clear that they expect parental involvement and provide a reasonable range of ways for parents to be involved, they should expect (and be rewarded by) greater involvement. If educators are persistent and patient, they will see positive changes over time. Involvement is a critical first step toward redefining the roles and responsibilities of parents in the educational process.

The Role of the Community

Educators often take a somewhat calculating perspective on the community's obligations to its public schools. Members of the community with no children in school traditionally have been viewed from a public relations perspective: How can they be encouraged to support schools financially? Other community institutions, such as businesses and governmental agencies, are often considered primarily as sources of donated goods or services. Members of these groups are beginning to expect more from schools and to be more questioning when their support is requested. Several suggestions of ways in which these groups might be involved in education follow.

Providing Learning Experiences in the World of Work. To succeed with all young people, particularly with those who have been disenchanted with traditional academic environments, schools may have to extend learning beyond the school site, on one hand, and bring many more adults into classrooms on the other. For this to occur, the community must become an active partner in education. Community here is defined broadly to mean all institutions, public and private, that have a stake in a well-educated citizenry and that may contribute to the educational experiences of young people.

Many community agencies and businesses may be asked to offer students opportunities to serve as interns or observers in the workplace. This will be a new and, for some, a problematic responsibility. Support, guidance, and financial incentive will need to be offered to those in the private sector to induce large-scale participation.

The movement to provide learning experiences outside schools may have to be developed gradually. The United States is not Germany, with its extensive (and expensive) youth apprenticeships. But programs that give students some experience in the world of work are a potentially powerful way to make school more relevant to students and to ease the transition from school to work.

Recent reports and writings suggest that the business community is becoming more aware of how difficult it is to change public schools. Many of these reports suggest that businesses must be prepared to be more involved for a sustained period of time if they are to influence public education. These writings suggest that it may be possible to begin the very basic and difficult changes in the relationship between schools and the community suggested here.

Providing Loaned Expertise to Schools. Community members can assist by offering their skills to schools. Many citizens possess content knowledge that is much more up-to-date than that of teachers. They can bring real-life problems into the school for students to solve, and they give students more opportunities to interact with and know adults in a positive light. They model what it is to be a productive member of society, and at the same time serve as a role model.

Letting Teachers and Administrators Work in Noneducational Settings in Structured Ways. Many educators have spent their entire lives in schools of one sort or another. They may have difficulty helping children relate what they are being taught to the world outside of the schools. One way to help overcome this is to bring adults from the work world into schools, as mentioned previously. The other is to give teachers the chance to spend time in the work world. Many teachers could benefit from and enjoy the chance to leave education for a period of time to participate in a different work environment.

There are many examples of such programs where students are provided opportunities to learn about the world of work. There are fewer designed to provide teachers with similar experiences. Schools and noneducational organizations can work together closely to provide structured programs of visitation and internship for teachers, during both the school year and the summer. Such programs invigorate teachers and enable them to align their curriculum and teaching methods more closely with the needs of society generally and the workplace more specifically.

For example, teams of teachers can conduct on-site visitations to local employers. During such a visitation, the teacher team interviews and observes different work groups within the company with two goals in mind: first, to understand how the curriculum in schools should be adapted to reflect the reality of the work world; and second, to get an idea of how adults organize themselves to work and produce in ways different from the ways in which a faculty is organized. Many teachers easily grasp this first reason and the need to address it. Fewer may initially see the need to consider different ways of structuring their own work environment. However, participants in activities like this come away with insights on both points that they can use to reshape their schools.

Sharing, Coordinating, and Combining Resources. Public agencies that serve youth can share resources in many more ways than they do currently. One area is facilities construction. Currently, each agency constructs its own facilities at great expense. These facilities are scattered throughout the community and may be located inconveniently for clients. A first step is to begin to construct new facilities collaboratively, or at least in a coordinated manner, and to consider some consolidation of facilities. The same concept holds true for transportation systems, which also may overlap. This type of coordination is politically very difficult, but in line with fiscal realities and expectations that public agencies become more efficient and productive in meeting client needs.

Other opportunities for sharing resources exist. Sometimes personnel can be shared among agencies, as between schools and parks or recreation departments. Similar arrangements with social welfare agencies are possible, although infrequently explored. Many schools are finding ways to house social welfare agency personnel at the school site to provide better service to students and to reduce the expectation that the school meets all of a student's needs.

Releasing Workers to Support Education. Business owners can be encouraged to support education by allowing employees to be released from work to visit the public schools, to adopt a school, to provide tutoring, or to visit their children's classrooms more regularly. Typically, both parents and nonparents participate in this type of program. They might go to school over lunch time, attend a special assembly, or mentor a troubled youth. They might make a presentation to a class, read a book to kindergarteners, or judge science projects.

Most workers would make up the time through flexible scheduling, or take the time off as compensation for hours worked beyond normal job requirements. Numerous companies have demonstrated that such arrangements can be accomplished with relative ease and minimal expense. One of the many benefits of such programs is that more people can experience the positive feelings associated with helping children to learn. Some employees miss having a chance to interact with young people, or the feeling that they are "making a difference" in the life of a child or of the community.

Creating Pressure for Fundamental Change in Education. Educators cannot be expected to transform schools without support and leadership from those outside schools. The role of parents as supporters of change has been mentioned. The larger community has a responsibility as well to be aware that schooling needs to change, and that to do so will be difficult.

A great deal of written material has been prepared that would help employers and employees understand the implications for the business community if schools don't change. Employers can make such materials available in the workplace. Business Roundtables in many states have attractive brochures and comprehensive reports detailing the need for educational improvement and change. Chambers of commerce and civic service clubs can devote time to presentations on the need for change in education, the possible solutions, and the role that members of their organization can play.

The net effect of these efforts can be to create broad-based awareness and acceptance of the need for educational change. Such a climate makes it more possible for local boards of education and school administrators to support, sustain, and initiate programs that reshape education and the community's role in schooling.

Being Involved in Site-Based Decision Making. Qualified members of the community can be valuable participants in groups such as site-based councils. Site-based councils will have more impact if energetic, diverse, and imaginative voices from outside the schools are included. Members of the business community can suggest many techniques for planning, analyzing data, redesigning programs, and becoming more customer sensitive. They potentially come to the table with less immediate self-interest than do many of the other groups that normally participate in such councils.

Serving as Judges for Student Demonstrations and Assessments. For those not inclined to participate in governance or other formal structures, schools can offer opportunities to participate without making a long-term, formal commitment. One example is to serve as a judge, or assessor, of student work. This does not mean grading papers. Instead, it means reviewing a project, performance, or written work against some clearly defined standard.

As states and school districts develop standards, there likely will be more widespread use of learning experiences like senior projects, capstone experiences, portfolios, and foreign language proficiency tests that require students to demonstrate publicly their ability to apply specified skills to meet certain standards. Judges will be needed because teachers cannot (and should not) do all the judging.

Community members add credibility to the judging. There is some external verification that the student work does meet the required standards. Students take such activities more seriously when they are being judged publicly by someone other than their teacher. Community participation can help educators see how the community believes students are meeting the required standards.

DISCUSSION QUESTIONS

1. What expectations do parents hold for the school currently?
2. How knowledgeable are parents about the school's instructional program and its standards for student performance?
3. Are parents an integral part of the school currently? What are the effects of parental involvement? Are there positive and negative aspects of parent involvement?
4. How would teachers and administrators view increased parent and community involvement?
5. What are the potential ways in which the local business community (private and public sector) could support student learning?
6. What is the proper relationship between the schools and local social service agencies?
7. How well do the schools coordinate their efforts with other public agencies that offer services to youth and families?

9 *Changing Roles of School Boards, Central Offices, and Teacher Associations*

Not much about schools will change if there are no changes in the groups responsible for establishing, interpreting, and implementing the rules under which schools operate. Local school boards and central office administrators can significantly influence the activities that take place at the school site. Teacher associations are equally influential in shaping the practices in most school districts. How can these groups get ready for restructuring? What do they need to do to make them ready to restructure, or to assist schools that are ready to restructure?

Boards of Education

In the United States, local school districts, about 15,500 in all, are accustomed to being able to operate with relative independence (when compared to local educational jurisdictions in other countries). Although some are more accountable than others, either to a regulatory-minded state department of education or an active community, few are prepared for the type of scrutiny to which they are likely to be subjected during the coming decade. Pressure for improved student performance is increasing. Resources are limited. Legislators are looking closely at schools. More groups want to be heard, and their voices are often shrill and partisan. Who is barring the door against the onslaught? The local school board stands poised to face some of the greatest challenges it has encountered in the past century.

The school board was designed initially as a guarantee that the local schools would transmit the values of the community effectively to the young, and that locally generated tax monies would be spent properly. The board was often an extension of church and local values in the early days of the republic. Boards became highly political as cities grew in the 1890s, then became the shining example of Progressive-era government reforms. After World War II, they became increasingly political again as organized interest groups challenged local boards to be responsive to their agendas.

Boards are changing again as school finance laws have moved funding to the state level, taking away the local board's ability to raise revenue. An emerging challenge is the movement to develop educational standards at the state and national levels, which would tend to limit board discretion in the instructional program. Stripped of authority in budgeting and instruction, the role of the local board becomes unclear and precarious.

At the same time, the board is expected to provide leadership for change. The impetus and rationale for this change frequently comes from the state, rather than the local, level. The board is caught in a crossfire of competing values and mandates. It may serve more as an arbitrator and referee than as the voice of leadership for the schools. Its authority limited, its constituents disaffected, its resources controlled externally, the board may find itself with little room to maneuver.

These challenges from outside the system are matched by challenges within. The movement to increased participation on school councils creates other groups of people making decisions within the district. The relationship between them and the board is often unclear, sometimes even tense. Why, the site council asks, should the board of education be able to overrule this decision if it has no effect on other schools? Why, the board asks, do we need school councils to make decisions best made by the board?

All of this suggests another change in the role of the board of education. If the state restricts board latitude, and individual schools continue to gain decision-making authority, the local boards of education might increasingly serve as a "board of directors" that helps set a general direction for the district, then reviews the plans, goals, and performances of the schools.

The school board acting as a board of directors might pay more attention to the "strategic direction" of the district, the performance of students, the development and periodic review of the district's performance standards, and budget development and approval within state guidelines. School sites consistently unable to meet their goals would be held accountable by the board of directors. The performance of the superintendent and key administrators would be reviewed periodically in light of improved student performance.

The board would return to one of its original functions, that of holding educators accountable for student performance, while abandoning the quasi-administrator role into which many boards have slipped. Boards may have brought on this problem by meeting too often. Board members may reject this conclusion out of hand because many feel that they can barely get through their agenda with weekly meetings that extend well into the night. In fact, this may be an indication that the board is too enmeshed in areas in which it should not be spending its time.

One intriguing notion is to have the board meet only three times a year, in much the same way that corporate boards of directors meet about that often. The primary purposes of these meetings would be to review, comment upon, modify, and approve proposed goals for the district and individual buildings; to assess the degree to which school and district goals were achieved; and to review and approve the proposed annual budget.

Obviously, such meetings would have to be longer than regular board meetings, perhaps taking up a Friday evening and all day Saturday. Most other decisions would be reallocated to management. The difference is that the board would be more willing to hold management accountable for these decisions. As it stands now, the board makes so many decisions that it is impossible to hold the administrative staff accountable, nor do administrators take much initiative.

There are obvious legal requirements that boards still have that would need to be addressed, including contract approval, some personnel decisions, and appeals of various disciplinary decisions. These responsibilities can be discharged in special sessions limited to the topic at hand, or executive sessions, where appropriate and legal.

Boards of education might be held in greater esteem if they were heard from less, but on more substantive issues. Meetings might be better attended and better covered by the media if they were more like town meetings or annual corporate board meetings.

Such an arrangement might make the role of board member more appealing. It might free the superintendent and central office staff to run the district on something less than a crisis basis, eliminating the biweekly (or weekly) panic within central office of preparing for, then reacting to, the board meeting. It might put more distance between the board and the professional staff than exists currently, allowing the board to be true citizen stewards, rather than having to meet with school administrators so much that the board starts to sound like administrators. It could be one more step toward loosening schools from constant oversight and micromanagement, a necessary first step toward allowing schools to restructure to improve student performance.

Central Administrators

There may be no other group whose role could be affected more profoundly by restructuring than central office administrators. Some seem to recognize the enormous challenges they face; others have not yet come to grips with the ways in which their role may be changing.

If more decisions are made at the school level, and student performance standards dictate the educational program for schools, central administrators will have to possess a new mixture of skills and responsibilities. Central administrators may be faced with a twofold challenge: Redefine their roles so that their contributions to improving student learning become clear, and develop the skills necessary to succeed in these newly defined roles. These skills are described in greater detail below.

Visionaries

One of the unanswered questions of decentralization is, How will people decide to do anything other than what they already do in the absence of some sense of clearly superior alternatives? Central office administrators should be key in helping develop the strategic directions of the district, the vision of a vastly improved educational system. This role requires administrators who are aware of current trends and issues in society and in education, who discuss, debate, and analyze these issues on a regular basis. In short, they have to think, create, dream, synthesize, analyze, and conceptualize.

Planners

Central office administrators may have more responsibility for guiding the organization through systematic planning activities. These activities would establish the district's direction and purpose. A plan like this is important because in the absence of a common plan that establishes shared vision, mission, and goals, there is little reason for schools to remain as a district, other than certain legal or economic reasons.

Identifying a common sense of purpose, or mission, and the ways in which everyone in the district can contribute to the mission can be done only by those in the center. To organize and oversee such a process successfully requires knowledge of planning models and skill in dealing with the interpersonal and political issues that surround planning.

Standard Setters

Central office administrators can play a key role in identifying performance standards in those districts that are developing standards. Where standards have been set by the state, the administrators can help schools interpret them. The central administration is responsible for communicating to parents how well each school is preparing students to meet required standards, and at the same time must be ready to help those schools that need assistance in understanding or making the transition to standards-based instruction. The central administration clarifies the ways in which schools are going to be accountable for student performance on required standards.

Facilitators

To a greater degree, central administrators may become facilitators of change, planning, implementation, dispute resolution, and interactions among all the groups in the district and community. Facilitation is the skill of supporting or enabling others to act on their own to solve problems or achieve their goals, as opposed to doing something for them (or to them). Facilitation works best when goals are known and shared; then central office administrators serve to help individuals or school sites achieve their goals.

The challenge is that facilitation requires a particular view of personal power. Those who view power as a way to control others will never be comfortable with facilitation. Furthermore, those who are not comfortable-with ambiguity and conflict will also shrink from the facilitator's role. Not every central office administrator will likely be suited to be a facilitator.

Boundary Spanners

Central office administrators move among schools in the district. They also have more opportunities to interact with the community at large. They may take advantage of the potential that such a perspective provides. They may be critical agents who work to build support for change within the larger community, and who identify emerging concerns about restructuring.

They can seek resources and strategic alliances. They can identify opportunities and link people in schools with these opportunities. They can create more communication between schools and the community. They can seek to find the common ground with other agencies in the community, so that all community agencies use their resources best to educate and develop young people.

Communicators

The need for central office administrators to communicate effectively through the written and spoken word seems obvious, on one hand. However, the ability to communicate is spread very unevenly among central office administrators currently, and the importance of effective communication skills is only likely to increase. This skill is necessary to communicate a vision, resolve problems, link schools together, and serve as a bridge to the community. Those who aspire to central office positions may need to demonstrate their competence, knowledge, clarity, and persuasiveness using verbal and written forms of communication before they are selected, and they may need to improve those abilities consistently while on the job.

Dispute Resolvers

As schools become more independent, central office administrators will be called upon more to settle disputes between schools. They may take on the role of "objective" external arbitrator. They will help all parties focus on improved performance by all schools when resolving disputes.

More conflict can be expected at schools and between schools, particularly as people make decisions somewhat in isolation from others in the district, and as they attempt to secure resources (money, facilities, etc.) for their schools. It is likely that the district will need people who can arbitrate between school sites when issues arise.

Efficiency Enhancers

There have been few incentives to make district offices more efficient. In a bureaucracy, more attention may be given to empire building than to efficiency. Education is very difficult to make efficient. Like most not-for-profit organizations, education tends to increase its size and demand for resources, without necessarily improving its performance.

Most states are expecting more efficient operation of schools and more money ending up in the classroom. This need for efficiency translates into fewer people in the central office. A central administrator will have to be an expert on alternative forms of service delivery and more efficient forms of organization to free up more resources to support student learning in schools.

Coordinators

The three different levels of elementary, middle, and high schools need to coordinate their efforts much better than they do currently if school districts use common performance standards to judge students. Central office administrators will be challenged to maintain a balance between the needs for consistency from grade to grade and school to school, on one hand, and for individuality and adaptation by school sites on the other. School site decision making tends to pull districts apart, whereas common standards dictate cooperation across levels and school sites. Striking the balance will be difficult.

The types of things that central office personnel might be expected to do more of in the future to improve coordination include

- Organizing and facilitating meetings across grade levels
- Analyzing the programs of individual school sites and identifying possible lacks of linkage between schools
- Identifying problems that may result from site-based decisions, looking for opportunities to infuse content across grade levels
- Spotting redundancies in school-based curricula

Moving to a Service-Based Model

If central office administrators embrace these roles and redesign the central office around service, they can create greater acceptance of and support for what they do. This service role of the central office makes it one more link in the chain, not the capstone of the pyramid. Learning to serve and lead at the same time will be a real change for administrators accustomed to issuing orders. The continued viability of the central office will hinge on the degree to which it functions as a resource for and partner to school improvement, rather than an obstacle to be circumvented.

Teachers' Unions

The role of teachers' unions (or associations) is beginning to change as well. They must retain the gains in "bread and butter" areas like salary and benefits while fulfilling the role of a professional association that is a partner in improving student learning.

During the past two decades, unions have concentrated first on wages and benefits, then on policy issues. They succeeded in getting better wages and benefits first, then were successful in getting many policy issues included in contracts. Topics such as class size limitations, teacher transfer rules, and other instructionally related issues began to appear in more contracts.

The role of teacher has evolved from worker toward professional. Teachers participate in decision making and program design to an ever-increasing degree. They design and approve staff development activities and district curriculum programs, teacher evaluation systems, and employment and retention of beginning teachers, to cite a few examples.

When teachers move beyond "labor," and administrators beyond "management," the stage is set for a new role for the teachers' union, not in place of bargaining for wages and benefits, but in addition to these areas. In many districts, the union has become an active partner in school improvement. This role can be difficult in some districts, particularly when the union is asked to help deal with the issue of poor-performing teachers, or of school reconstitution, where an entire faculty is transferred out of a school and a new one hired. However, many teachers are expecting their organization to do more than bargain wages and benefits. They are asking that it be a tool for professional development and school improvement.

Some teachers' unions have begun to sponsor teacher networks and workshops, to support radical school restructuring programs, and to train teachers how to change their schools. Some key union leaders have become national and regional spokespeople for school reform. Local unions have more opportunities to sit as equals in the school restructuring process. They can participate in planning and implementing such programs of change.

Some unions recognize that their members' needs have changed. Many districts have not hired new teachers for years, and the average age has increased to the point where union members are veterans at or beyond mid-career. These teachers seek ways to revitalize their careers. They want to feel they are effective in their jobs as much as they want a 3% pay increase. Many are frustrated and burned out with the current model of schooling.

Unions recognize this and adopt a more flexible stance when working with boards of education and administrators. They continue to represent the legitimate interests of teachers through a wider range of strategies, including collaborative problem solving, joint labor-management standing committees, task forces, pilot programs, contract waivers at individual school sites when approved by faculty, and agreements to leave school restructuring out of the contract.

School districts are unlikely to change dramatically without redefined roles for boards, central administrators, and unions. These key players establish the ground rules within which changes at school sites can occur. Creating readiness among people in these roles will be challenging because they may believe they have much to lose by any changes to the current way of doing things.

These same people also know better than anyone the limitations and frustrations of the current system. They may be ready to try something else because it is clear if they continue to do what they have always done, schools will be unable to adapt to a changing world and to improve student learning dramatically.

DISCUSSION QUESTIONS

1. Which decisions are best made by boards of education? Which are best made by site councils? Which by central office? Which by principals?

2. How can boards of education enable schools to restructure? What limits should they place on schools? How should they hold schools accountable?

3. What would a service-oriented central office look like? What are the major things that would need to be changed?

4. What is the proper role for a teachers' union in the restructuring process?

PART IV

How Can a School
Begin to Restructure?

10 *Building Readiness for Restructuring*

Readiness is rarely addressed systematically as a part of the change process. This book is designed to help do just that. Preceding chapters have raised a series of issues designed to focus teachers, administrators, parents, and community members on whether they agree on the need to change their schools. This chapter now refocuses the discussion on what the school should do once there is some level of acceptance by faculty and community of the need to change and some agreement on the need to build readiness.

Many school leaders and innovators appear to misjudge and underestimate the amount of time and energy that must be spent nurturing readiness. These leaders have already adjusted their worldview and accommodated themselves to the changes they are proposing. More important, they see how they will succeed, or at least survive, after the changes have taken place. They can anticipate and understand most of the predictable effects of the proposed changes. They have already adjusted their mental model of the world to accommodate what they are proposing. Why, they wonder, doesn't everyone else understand all of this as they do?

For many, perhaps most, of the people in a school who are being asked to change, this level of awareness simply does not exist, nor can it exist without difficulty. Readiness is not achieved by simply providing information to participants and answering their questions regarding how the changes will affect them.

Ultimately, all participants need the opportunity to examine their current thinking, beliefs, and practices at a different, more fundamental level. They need to be given the opportunity to understand the rationale for change and the broader framework within which the proposed change exists. Readiness activities are those that allow participants to have the opportunity to reshape their mental model, their worldview, to accommodate the proposed changes, and, most important, to understand how the changes benefit students and how participants will be able to survive and succeed after the changes are in place.

To do so, they need to see and experience different models. They need to be aware of new, unexplored possibilities. They need to have the barriers and isolation that typifies schools broken down. They need to have their assumptions challenged by seeing schools that operate successfully with different assumptions. They need to have the chance to develop a wider worldview. They need the chance to develop new solutions and to adopt what might be described as a "systems" perspective.

The following sections discuss some ways to help people get ready for restructuring, beginning with visits to other schools and work sites as a way to begin developing a new sense of what is possible and desirable.

Building Readiness by Visiting Other Schools

One effective means of increasing readiness is to provide staff with the opportunity to visit schools that are actively involved in restructuring. Sometimes, these observations strengthen the visitors' resolve to change their own schools; other times, they leave educators wondering why they even bothered to visit the site. Such visits can give educators a better sense of how (and why) their school should change its practices, or can lead to a rejection of restructuring. Without careful selection of visitation sites and proper preparation for those who visit, the value of such visits is greatly diminished. However, when they are effective, school visits can have very powerful effects at a personal level.

Visitors must look beneath the surface to understand the effects of restructuring. Understanding why people chose to do what they did can be as valuable as understanding what it is they are doing. It is particularly difficult to observe learning taking place. The learning process is elusive. Teachers often talk about how they seek "the teachable moment." What is the likelihood of observing one on any given visit?

However, a careful visitor can learn to see beyond the immediate events and activity of the classroom, be it immaculate or cluttered, beyond the "official" descriptions of the school offered by the host, beyond any prepared written materials that extol the program by describing the ideal version of it, to learn valuable lessons and glean useful ideas, both in terms of what to do and what not to do.

Here are some examples of things to look for when visiting a school engaged in restructuring or any major change:

- A clear emphasis on improved student learning as the ultimate goal of the restructuring program, and a way to document success, not just progress
- The ability of teachers and students to describe what they are doing that is different from what they used to do, and why they are doing it
- Evidence that all or nearly all of the students are productively engaged in learning and understand what is expected of them
- Evidence that the restructuring program extends beyond a few teachers, classrooms, or one program in the school
- Students who are enthusiastic and excited and who can explain the program's strengths and weaknesses
- An effective system for tracking student progress in a new way consistent with the program's (or school's) restructuring goals
- A comfortable atmosphere and a relationship of trust and respect between learners and adults
- A physical environment that suggests that the people in it have some sense of community or belonging

Other, less tangible things to look for include the following:

- Evidence of buy-in among most staff, not just the innovators
- Parental involvement in program design and functioning
- Community support for the program
- A rational process by which agreement was reached on the program, including some reference to research or evidence that the program is likely to be effective
- The ability to conduct the program or approach within the school's existing resource base, if not now then at some identified time in the future

- Evidence that the program is not so dependent on one individual that it is unlikely that anyone else could duplicate the effort
- The amount of time and skill necessary to conduct the program; is it such that average faculty would be incapable or quickly burned out?

Given the relative openness of schools to visits, there is potentially much to be gained through visiting other schools. Visitors will gain much if they do not expect to see schools that have solved all of education's problems, but have taken a solid first step toward a new vision of teaching and learning. Because schools tend to follow the "early innovators," the activities of the many "lighthouse" schools making early strides in restructuring are important to observe and to learn from when working to create readiness.

Visiting Sites Other Than Schools

As valuable as visits to schools are, they rarely cause teachers to move too far outside their current views of schooling. They remain within their comfort zone while visiting and can be quite judgmental about their colleagues at other schools. An additional way to expose teachers to new ideas is to have them visit settings totally outside the educational system. The most likely candidates are businesses and governmental agencies.

A visit to a business can be an eye-opening experience for teachers. Most of them like getting a look at how "the other half" lives, and most come away feeling more secure about themselves as professionals because "business doesn't have all the answers." At the same time, teachers tend to learn a great deal from a properly structured visit.

Setting up a visitation takes careful planning. First, the right setting must be selected. Generally, this is a company that has redesigned itself into work teams, that demonstrates how business is becoming global, that is innovative in the way it structures time or other aspects of work, that develops its employees, or that has in some way rethought the traditional ways to organize people. Furthermore, it must be a site where at least one key person is very interested in education generally, and preferably in education reform or restructuring specifically.

Most visits involve tours and discussions between teachers and company personnel, but many go beyond this model. Some companies allow teachers to work alongside their employees, if only for the day. Others rotate the teachers through a series of tasks within the company. When a company has its own corporate trainers, it may have them discuss their worker and management training programs with educators to see how each approaches the task of teaching. Personnel directors can have teachers take the tests and fill out the forms that job applicants would complete, or learn about the difficulties that employees have and how prospective employees could be better prepared to help them avoid these difficulties.

Generally, all of these activities would be 1 or 2 days in length. There are other options that extend to a week or more. One company rotates several teachers through all the basic job levels in the organization over the course of a summer and requires the teachers to present to the CEO of the company a report summarizing their observations and making recommendations to improve the company. Other short-term internships pair teachers with employees to work jointly on a specific report or study that they complete in the allotted amount of time. Each contributes her or his expertise, each is valued, and the teacher comes to understand the dynamics of the company firsthand. In turn, the company comes to appreciate the skills of educators.

All visitations, whether short or long, require some sort of summary debriefing at the end of the day or period of time. In most cases, the teachers produce a report on the spot or shortly thereafter summarizing their insights and observations in two categories, as they relate to (a) what students should know and (b) how faculty and staff could be organized best to meet their job requirements and student needs. These reports are shared with the host and with other teachers at the school. Observations common to the reports are captured with the goal of injecting them into discussions about restructuring at the school.

Some Other Strategies for Building Readiness

There are many other ways that readiness can be increased. In general, all of the strategies attempt to get people to think, analyze, and apply different perspectives to their current situation. Remember that most educators have spent the better part of their lives in schools (and have done reasonably well in them), and you will understand how important and difficult it is to get them simply to think about how things could be different.

Most of the suggestions I offer here are not revolutionary. However, they are rarely employed systematically to build readiness. The general strategies I suggest include

- Study groups
- Task forces
- Collecting data about the school and sharing it (profiling)
- Book discussion groups
- Articles about effective educational methods and models
- Abstracts of articles
- Thought-provoking materials including examples of programs
- Binders organized into sections where teachers put articles on new programs and ideas, the contents of which are shared periodically
- Attendance at conferences, retreats, and special events
- Yearly events like retreats or other times where faculty and community come together and step back from day-to-day issues to consider the "big picture"
- Regular time at faculty meetings to consider new ideas

Many of these activities are currently attempted only sporadically and are not linked to any systematic effort to change. They are more effective when linked and when several are going on at any given time. Their power should not be underestimated. They can subtly reshape the culture of the school, establish new norms of participation, and reduce isolation because they create many opportunities for people to talk with one another and exchange ideas and points of view. These are the first crucial steps—decreased isolation, increased collegiality, and an expanding worldview. If growth is occurring in these three areas, a school can state with some confidence that it has taken concrete steps to build readiness for change.

Pitfalls to Watch for
When Beginning the Restructuring Process

There are definite pitfalls in moving away from the safety and predictability of the current way of doing things toward the more uncertain future presented by restructuring. Many of the early innovators in school restructuring have been surprised at just how many obstacles there are. For anyone getting ready to restructure, the following nine pitfalls can help to anticipate some of the more or less inevitable bumps along the road.

Pitfall 1: Lack of a Vision. Many schools approach change in a piecemeal fashion, developing a series of fragmented activities that responds to specific concerns, often those held by a vocal minority of the faculty. Sometimes, the school adopts the latest trends or techniques. Restructuring becomes a series of unrelated, unconnected projects, activities, or changes in the organizational structure. Nothing holds these projects together. Few people see where the school is going in the long run, or how one change already undertaken might suggest another one not yet fully defined. Innovative projects then get subjected to near-microscopic scrutiny by skeptics.

The importance of pursuing some sort of general consensus about where the school is going and why cannot be stressed enough. Teachers operate so independently and in such isolation that it is especially important for them to have a shared sense of purpose and direction. A common mission helps everyone align his or her efforts toward agreed-upon ends and, as a by-product, reduces resistance among those who resist specific programs.

Pitfall 2: The Time Trap. There is never enough time in education. It is easy for a faculty to become sidetracked on one issue and spend most of its time spinning its wheels trying to resolve a very small issue. Successful schools direct their energies toward those activities most likely to yield changes and improvements.

At the same time, they acknowledge that it takes time to implement new practices, usually several years, and that during the implementation phase, efficiency and performance may actually decrease. This period can be critical because teachers may return to former ways. Collegial support combined with awareness of how difficult it is to change seem to be key elements in helping people through the "implementation dip," that short-term decrease in performance that can accompany a change in the established way of doing things.

The time trap also has the tendency to burn out highly motivated people, those who emerge to pioneer programs and to fill newly created leadership roles. They become emotionally invested in the vision, and they work exceedingly hard to turn it into a reality. However, they are at risk of being overwhelmed by the combination of regular work responsibilities, new duties, and their life outside of school. Care must be exercised to ensure that these people have the time necessary to be successful, and that they are encouraged to take an occasional break. The only realistic way to accomplish this is to spread leadership roles around, thereby building collegiality and encouraging the sharing of responsibilities and tasks. Many people who have never shown interest in or aptitude toward leadership may contribute in unexpected ways if allowed to do so.

Most important, time must be available for people to talk about and understand the reasons for the change. This time is separate from any time necessary for staff training. Teachers simply need to be able to talk with one another and with parents and community members, not about grades or problems with Johnny, but about the goals of the school, the realities of students' lives, and the world outside of schools. They need to compare notes, to see that they are not alone, that their problems are shared by others, and that the solutions may not be as simple as they first thought. They need time to reach the conclusion that they might have to abandon some cherished practices and adopt new and different techniques or ways of thinking. They need to become comfortable sharing ideas with and learning from others.

Pitfall 3: Proceeding Without the Community. It is very easy for educators to overlook the larger community when they undertake change. Community members should be involved from the beginning in the process of vision building and in all the readiness-building activities described in this book.

Schools should be more willing to publicize their proposed programs of restructuring earlier and broadly. Although there is a risk that too much said too soon might needlessly alarm parents, this should be balanced against the consequences of not consulting with key community groups and influential leaders before moving forward on something as simple as a change in the schedule.

A willingness to go to the community is important. Coffees in parents' homes, where issues can be raised and discussed informally, are simultaneously important and underused platforms to sound out and inform the community. Quality written materials need to accompany any such meeting. Brief, informal, informative brochures that answer frequently asked or easily anticipated questions must be readily available.

Pitfall 4: Questions of Meaning. The lack of a common definition of the term *restructuring* has been both a blessing and a curse—a blessing in that it has allowed groups as disparate as teachers' unions and school boards to align themselves in a common cause, at least in principle, and a curse because people can do almost anything and claim that they are restructuring. This "anything goes" mentality has tended to devalue the term and has led many educators to view it with a mixture of caution and cynicism.

Observations in schools engaged in restructuring suggest that teachers and administrators in these schools do not spend a great deal of time debating the meaning of restructuring; these educators do believe, however, that changes must go beyond the superficial. This shared belief expands and is honed as concrete issues of practice are confronted, analyzed, and resolved. A definition of restructuring is built "on the fly" and modified the same way.

In the alternative, a school can reach agreement about key terms and concepts so that everyone knows what *block scheduling* or *nongraded primary* means. It is dangerous to assume that everyone understands what these terms mean. Community members in particular may have wildly differing interpretations of what a term like *nongraded primary* means. Even the basic notion of restructuring can be defined usefully beforehand if readiness has been developed.

Pitfall 5: Rose-Colored Glasses Syndrome. When restructuring is viewed as a series of projects, it is common for principals in particular to miscalculate the amount of time and energy necessary to achieve meaningful, sustained change and the amount of resistance such a process engenders. Perhaps this is why an outsider sees little substantial change in many schools that describe themselves as restructured. Those involved see what they want to see.

Rose-colored glasses can be a plus at times. They help people get involved and committed. But many early innovators find themselves overwhelmed and surprised at the negative reactions that their ideas engender. Enthusiasm tempered with a healthy dose of reality might be the best combination for individuals and teams embarking on school change projects of any magnitude.

Pitfall 6: Changes in Governance as Ends in Themselves. Many school districts apparently believed that new ways of making decisions alone would magically transform education, unleashing a pent-up torrent of ideas and programs for improvement. Things have not worked out that way to date.

Instead, many faculties are bogged down in the minutiae of participatory decision making without knowing why it was instituted or what purpose it is supposed to serve. In many cases, site-based decision making is a solution in search of a problem. In the absence of real reasons for teachers to make decisions or substantial resources for them to control, they make decisions in areas such as how to supervise the buses, what day an early release should be scheduled, or how students should line up for class pictures. Changes in governance structure should be undertaken to achieve and support improvement of student learning only. If the governance structures do not help this to happen, they should be examined and modified to get their focus onto improving student learning.

Pitfall 7: Measuring New Learning With Old Tools. Schools adopt programs that pursue new goals for learning, such as problem solving and critical thinking. At the same time, they continue to rely on standardized achievement test scores or similar measures as the only way they judge their success.

Finding new ways to assess student learning is the first part of the problem. And although it is a definite issue, it is not as difficult as many assume. The quality and variety of alternative assessment methods and instruments is rapidly increasing. The second part is getting local communities to accept the results of these assessments as valid indicators of student learning. If schools do not put both elements of this equation into place, they are forced to use old tools to measure their effectiveness and success against old benchmarks.

Schools must be ready to pay attention to how they will assess student learning at the same time that they consider adopting new teaching methods, curricula, schedules, or grouping strategies. When restructuring programs are being designed, decisions on how students will be assessed need to be made at the same time.

Pitfall 8: Analysis Paralysis. One of the striking features of the current interest in school restructuring is the number of schools that have established "restructuring committees" or some other group charged with investigating whether or not (or how) to change. Many, perhaps most, of these committees are composed of teachers who are excited by the prospects for change. They read articles, discuss and debate, meet with experts and consultants, and visit other schools. They develop a very good understanding of the issues that face their school and the options available for improving the school.

The moment of truth arrives when it is time for the faculty to respond to the recommendations or observations of the committee. Will faculty choose to act, or will they want to continue to study the process before they make a decision? Very often, faculties choose to postpone a decision on the committee's recommendations. The recommendations are not voted down or rejected out of hand; instead, faculty request more information or study before agreeing to any changes. The net result is to study the situation to death. The energy and enthusiasm for change dissipate before any meaningful action is undertaken. The storm subsides, and the school continues along the path of the status quo with its rationale for not changing firmly intact.

One way to help avoid this pitfall is to gain prior agreement about what will be done with the committee's recommendations. At the very least, an agreement to vote them up or down will head off analysis paralysis. In the meantime, the initiators of change have a responsibility to work informally before such a vote to take into account the concerns and unanswered questions of the skeptics and the perpetually nervous. Quiet work to address their concerns, or at least to anticipate them, helps the school to continue moving forward. It is also wise to have at least one of them on the committee.

Pitfall 9: Isolating the Innovators. The previous pitfall illustrates the difficulty that innovators have in traditional school settings. Whereas some are frustrated by being trapped in the analysis loop, others are literally physically segregated in one program or area of the building. The tendency of schools to "wall off" innovators the way the body does an invading cell sometimes takes the shape of the school-within-a-school. The innovators are free to pursue their own goals and practices while the rest of the faculty is left in peace. This can create the appearance of significant change, whereas most of the school remains unchanged. Visitors are escorted to the innovative program down hallways where they pass classroom after classroom where nothing has changed.

Changes can profitably begin in one part of the school if the program can function as a sort of "research and development" center within the school, where new ideas can be tried, refined, and modeled for the rest of the faculty. This strategy will work only in places where all faculty agree that the lessons learned in these settings will be applied to the total school program eventually.

Getting such an agreement is not always easy. Most teachers are content to allow their colleagues to engage in experiments as long as they themselves are not compelled to change as a result of such experiments. If restructuring is to occur, the work of innovative, pioneering teachers that proves successful in improving student learning must have an effect on the total school program eventually. If this does not occur, these pioneers will burn out, and the traditional structure will reassert itself by swallowing up the school-within-a-school.

These observations on the pitfalls of restructuring emphasize the difficulty of change within schools. The challenges and pitfalls on the road to restructuring presented in this chapter are daunting. In the next chapter, I offer some suggestions on how to understand and perhaps influence three critically important elements that can be aligned to support readiness. These are culture, commitment, and vision.

DISCUSSION QUESTIONS

1. Where is the school currently in terms of readiness?
2. How bureaucratic is the school? In what ways is it a learning community?
3. Which strategies for building readiness would be most appropriate in this school?
4. Which of the pitfalls to restructuring should the school be most aware of if it restructures? Why? How can the pitfall be anticipated?

11 *Creating Alignment for Restructuring*

Even though change is difficult, it is not impossible. There are things that administrators and teachers can do to nurture the general conditions that support change. In this chapter, I discuss how to cultivate a number of elements that can work in combination to create and capitalize upon readiness for restructuring. Three important factors can be managed with considerable impact: culture, commitment, and vision.

Culture

Basically, the culture of a school is the way people think about things, the way they do things, and the way they interact based on those beliefs and activities—all the rules and roles, formal and informal. It is how people treat one another, how they think about their role in the larger group, how they handle conflict and celebration, and how they communicate—the rituals and myths, the collective history, and the storytelling and gossiping. The process of school restructuring cannot be thought of simply as changes in the structures and programs of schools, or as isolated projects and activities. Ultimately, restructuring affects the culture of the school, and that culture can make or break any attempt at large-scale change.

Understanding the importance and power of culture can help educational leaders anticipate and attend to the needs that people are sure to have in times of rapid change. When leaders change, when familiar routines or rituals are disrupted, when roles are redefined, the culture changes. This creates stress for many people, and they do not know why, nor do they necessarily know how to handle the emotions that they are experiencing. When the changes occur in stable organizations, such as schools, they evoke even more powerful psychological responses. Even talk of restructuring can quickly raise anxiety levels to near the breaking point.

School leaders need to be capable of reading school culture if they hope to create readiness for fundamental change. Good ideas are rarely implemented simply because they make sense. Rather, schools tend to accept ideas or programs that are consistent with their existing structure, assumptions, and culture. For example, a school that "believes" that not all students can learn is more receptive to programs that rely on ability grouping than a school that believes all students can learn.

There are many specific areas to consider when managing change in a school's culture. The history of the school must be recognized and taken into account along with its current view of itself, the community's view of it, and the match between the two. Changes in student population or community demographics are also crucial. The ways in which people communicate formally and informally their stated and unstated beliefs, values, and assumptions must be understood and acknowledged. Formal and informal leadership structures and school micropolitics will affect how change is processed. The school's perception of itself as an innovative or traditionalist environment comes into play. Recent traumatic events, such as the loss of a beloved leader or faculty member, a strike, the closing of a building, or a layoff of teachers must be acknowledged and their influence considered when assessing culture and preparing for major change.

Leadership is required to oversee this complex process. A leader's job is to make conscious decisions that have an impact on the culture of the school in ways that make that culture more amenable to changes that improve student learning.

Successful leaders reshape culture by first establishing a bedrock understanding of the culture and then working to build readiness to change the culture. They identify the elements of the culture that they must confront and those that can be used to their advantage in preparing the school for change.

Several basic strategies help leaders manage culture to support restructuring. They maintain extensive informal communication networks throughout the school. They master the power and value of personal symbolic behavior. They acknowledge the limits of their power and come to understand how they are perceived. They identify the storytellers, historians, scribes, and keepers of the legends. They create public events, rituals, celebrations, and ceremonies that promote new cultural values. They create new roles, new leaders, and new rewards while carefully acknowledging the contributions of the "old guard." They use language carefully to motivate and guide emerging new cultural values, and they acknowledge the passing of the familiar in appropriate ways that allow mourning and a moving on to the new.

Principals are in a unique position to provide the leadership to modify school culture and guide the change process. However, many principals worry about the effects that such changes will have on their role. They are unable to see how they will be successful in a school where they may not be at the center of power. Because principals can make or break innovations, they must see how they can be winners in any restructured system. One way is to function as an effective leader and manager of cultural change.

Creating Commitment
for Restructuring

A fundamental question to be asked before restructuring activities begin is whether the school can tolerate such a challenging, arduous process. Many times, a highly motivated leader or group of leaders within a school has pushed strongly for a school to restructure in spite of the wishes of most staff and community members. Although there is sometimes reason to be a "voice in the wilderness," particularly in situations where faculty are so self-satisfied that they are unlikely ever to change, there is also danger. The backlash can be so strong that it delays serious self-examination of a school's assumptions and practices for several years or more. Such a backlash can even eliminate the word *restructuring* and related concepts from the school's collective vocabulary. Other schools are so fragile or damaged that they cannot survive rapid change; they overload and essentially collapse.

One way to avoid the possibility of a backlash or collapse is to begin by discussing general ground rules for change. This method allows the faculty and community to explore the implications of change before beginning the process itself. This is important because discussions of ground rules are not the same as discussions of specific changes in programs. Once change gets specific, someone generally is threatened. Even though everyone may have agreed at some point to some proposed change, behaviors (and recollections of what was agreed upon) often are quite different when it is time to implement the agreed-upon change. Spending the time to discuss whether the faculty or school community would be willing to commit to a series of principles that guides restructuring gives individuals a forum in which to raise concerns and fears. At the same time, the shift in culture starts to occur as the school moves toward a stronger sense of common purpose.

The following ten statements are examples of the types of commitments that come out of such a forum. These statements might be used by a school's faculty as the starting point to consider whether they are ready and willing to embark upon a challenging process of self-examination. The statements, which I call the Ten Commitments, can cause staff to reflect on their values, the school's culture, and the process to be followed if the school chooses to restructure. They are written here in the form of agreements, with brief accompanying descriptions of what staff would be committing specifically to do.

I should note that almost any set of commitments is better than no commitments, and that there is nothing magical about those mentioned here. Furthermore, it is useful to examine the degree of commitment and the types of commitment that each of these statements implies. Doing so can suggest how far a faculty is willing to go. All of the commitments that follow probably would be agreed to only in those schools most willing to engage in serious reflection and redesign. Realistically, most schools might find themselves able to start by agreeing upon several of these statements initially. Even if agreement is not reached on a particular commitment, the discussions can nevertheless be informative.

1. We commit to using data to make decisions. Faculty will employ information on current school processes and student performance, best educational practices, and societal trends as their frame of reference when making decisions. Data will be collected to identify what is working at the school along with what is not. Faculty will acquire the skills necessary to collect and analyze data. Once data are collected and analyzed, they will be shared before decisions are made. This requires time to collect and analyze data and a commitment to discuss the implications of the data and to consider a range of possible causes and responses. This commitment generally means the school must also commit to using a systematic planning model for a sustained period of time.

2. We commit to creating and sustaining a culture in the school that supports greater self-knowledge, professional development, and experimentation. In many schools, some of this happens in pockets of the school, but rarely is it the norm for the entire faculty. In a school undergoing restructuring, faculty begin by examining the school's practices, then creating professional growth activities that enable staff to develop new skills or improve existing ones to meet needs identified in the review of current practices. Additionally, staff must allow a variety of programs to be tested to see what works best with the school's culture and clientele. Openness to carefully controlled experimentation helps the school select and incorporate new approaches and programs.

3. We commit to accepting that there are aspects of the learning environment that prevent or limit student learning. In many schools, there is a tendency to make individual learners responsible for their lack of success in school. Sometimes, this responsibility is appropriate. On other occasions, failure is attributed to the child's home environment or economic class, or perhaps unconsciously to the child's race or sex. All these explanations end up removing the school from a position of responsibility for student success. Although many children do bring difficult, almost intractable problems to school, a faculty must decide if it is going to accept these as reasons why all students cannot be expected to learn.

This commitment means in essence that the school will design an instructional program that does everything possible to help each student succeed before the learner is identified as the problem. The school will alter its design and practices to accommodate the realities of its clients' lives before the clients can be blamed.

4. We commit to viewing children as human beings first, students second. In the final analysis, the most vital and important activities in education are those that occur during face-to-face interactions between teachers and students. Technology, innovative schedules, governance structures, and teaching materials are not a substitute for quality relationships between caring adults and motivated children. The ability to transmit content knowledge alone is not enough. Students more than ever need to know that the teacher cares about them before they care what the teacher knows.

Will the faculty be willing to assess the ways in which the school treats students? Does the school allow adults and students to develop relationships based on mutual respect? Do the rules and procedures that are used to control student behavior create more problems than they solve? Are some children isolated and invisible within the school? What does the school look and feel like from the student's point of view? Particularly in secondary schools, does the content come to dominate the learning experience so much that students and teachers do not engage at any level other than that needed to transmit and process content knowledge?

5. We commit to using a wide range of teaching methods. The students found in today's schools require a broader range of teaching methods than did students 40 years ago. Studies have found that most students spend the vast majority of their time either listening to lectures, doing seatwork, or following directions. If a faculty commits to using a wider range of teaching techniques, more students will experience a variety of ways to learn. Many of these techniques will involve students more in learning. Strategies such as cooperative learning, project-centered learning, debates and simulations, demonstrations and labs, and field-based learning all engage students actively. These techniques capture the interest of many students who would otherwise be bored and turned off to school.

Will teachers be ready to develop new skills? Many have already attended training sessions but have not put their newly learned methods into practice. Will they do so now? Will the school change in the ways necessary to allow teachers to use new methods successfully? Will schedules be modified? Will it be possible to leave campus to learn in the community? Will interdisciplinary learning be possible? Will teachers be able to work in teams to support one another and plan together? Expanding the range of teaching techniques requires first, that they be learned; second, that they be accommodated and supported; and third, that they be put into practice.

6. We commit to eliminating or phasing out those elements of our program that are not the best and most appropriate learning experiences for our students. This commitment is very difficult for educators to make because eliminating any program or task generally means hurting a colleague. That is why it is very important to make a distinction between eliminating a program and eliminating a person. Schools should seek to value each staff member while examining the value of each program separately.

Very often, the individuals who might be affected are highly skilled and dedicated; the problem is that what they teach may no longer be the best use of either the teacher's or students' time. Particularly as the resources allocated to education shrink, it becomes more necessary to make difficult choices between the programs to retain and the programs to alter or eliminate. Are schools capable of making such decisions internally, or must they rely on outside forces to do this for them?

It is easier to wait to be told to eliminate a program when the result might affect a colleague negatively. However, jobs might be saved if the school anticipated likely cuts and begins restructuring their programs before cuts had to be made. Teachers should be retrained before a program is replaced, rather than after it is eliminated. In this way, these adults are honored, and it is made clear that they are still valued members of the organization.

7. We commit to including parents and community members as equal partners in the education of children. Most educators agree with this in principle. In practice, however, parental participation in many schools is strictly optional and at the discretion of individual teachers. Are staff members willing to develop schoolwide expectations for parental involvement in the classroom? Are they willing to give parents more ways to support their child's education at home? Are they willing to expect parents to be members of a team with the common goal of educating the child?

The commitment to include parents and community members and to be more accountable to them has to be nurtured and developed in many concrete ways, particularly in those places where parents have not been involved and where social conditions make education difficult. Are staff willing to do all the things that are necessary to regain parent trust and involvement, to make them feel welcome at school, to provide them with the information they need to be stronger partners, and to listen to their complaints and criticisms, however difficult it may be to do so? Are parents willing to assume clearer responsibility for supporting the school? Are community members and agencies ready to shoulder their share of the burden?

8. We commit to involving staff in decisions that set the direction for change in the school. Schools cannot be restructured without the active cooperation of teachers and other staff. Simply changing the way in which decisions are made generally does not transform a school. But it is equally clear that schools will not change if staff members are not involved in key decisions. They must take ownership of and responsibility for increasing student success and for redesigning the school if this goal can be achieved.

With this in mind, it is important for all staff members to have the opportunity to be involved in decisions that will change the way they work and the expectations that are held for them. This commitment assumes a genuine desire by administration to respect the decisions made and to build upon them as the basis for restructuring.

Unfortunately, some people use participation as a way to obstruct change. Participation should not become a license to stop change altogether. Will the process serve to move change forward, not to stall it in endless debate and discussion? Will decisions move the school forward, or will they create the illusion of movement while ensuring that little actually changes? Constructive participation linked with commitment to change is key to solving the restructuring puzzle.

9. We commit to establishing a shared vision and set of goals for the school. Evidence that many schools lack clear purpose or direction seems to be mounting at the same time that the need for purpose and direction increases. Much of what occurs in schools is unconnected or even contradictory, particularly when viewed from the students' perspective. Many students cannot really state the reasons that they attend school; they don't know why they are there.

Schools have been content simply to maintain themselves from year to year. They have not worried much about whether they are improving or meeting student needs better. Are staff willing to spend the time and make the commitment to identify shared beliefs and values, then develop a common direction to achieve goals that reflect an agreement on the purposes of an education? Are they willing to establish clear goals, based on the vision and focused on improving student learning, then hold the school accountable for achieving them? Are they willing to set aside their personal agendas and make decisions and judgments based on the vision and goals? Are they willing to alter the school's structure and programs to achieve the vision and goals? Are they willing to allocate resources accordingly?

10. We commit to helping adults who are threatened or challenged by changes occurring in the school. In return, all adults in the school agree to be supportive or constructively critical once decisions have been made openly. It is not reasonable to ask people to change if they will be worse off as a result of having done so. Yet when schools restructure, many of the changes have more of an effect on some staff than on others. Some will be expected to develop new skills, teach in new ways or in new areas, or interact differently with students. Some may find their current programs or responsibilities eliminated. Others may find that their role in the culture or leadership structure may change dramatically.

Will the organization commit to providing support to those staff for whom change will be especially difficult or challenging? Will an effort be made to ensure that staff will not be asked to do things or make decisions that are against their own best interests? Will all current staff be guaranteed continuing employment somewhere in the district and assistance in adapting?

If support is provided, the school may ask in return that all staff help achieve the new goals and programs, or publicly voice constructive criticism or raise questions with the goal of improving the process. Staff can be expected either to support the changes that have to be made or to suggest how better to accomplish these aims.

Open, participatory decision making (as specified in the eighth commitment) provides a forum within which concerns can and must be aired. But concerned staff must state their positions openly. It is not acceptable to remain silent throughout a participatory decison-making process and then to work against the decisions that are made. Setting this ground rule can help diffuse much of the tension that arises after a decision has been made. This tension can sabotage educational restructuring efforts.

These commitments represent the first step in translating readiness into action. The next step is to arrive at some level of agreement about the broad outlines of restructuring, the overall goal, the destination of the journey. That step is taken when a school community works on a clear vision or set of goals that members can understand, support, and are committed to pursuing.

Creating the Vision

Change in education has generally resulted in training teachers in a particular program or curriculum. As such, change has been viewed as a process of sharpening teachers' existing skills. By contrast, restructuring may demand that schools pursue new goals or be redesigned in ways that are quite different. This level of change requires staff to understand and commit to the overall goals of the process, not merely to participate in isolated training activities. Such commitment is unlikely to be developed when teachers have little understanding of or input into the overall goals, purposes, and direction of the school. Vision-building creates an opportunity for such involvement to occur.

In many respects, readiness for restructuring primarily begins not by identifying new programs, but by developing a new picture in people's minds of what schooling should look like. Such a picture generally contains values, beliefs, assumptions, and practices that, taken as a whole, constitute a new vision of education. This is often referred to as the school's vision.

The term *vision* has appeared with increasing frequency in both the private and public sector. There seems to be the assumption—mistaken, I believe—that everyone in a school knows what vision is and what the implications are if a school has committed to a vision. Before a sense of vision can guide and motivate educators, school personnel must have a better understanding of what it is, how it can be developed, and what can be accomplished by its use.

Vision is not a term that is easily defined or understood. In some respects, people respond to the concept the same way they do to art: They can't define it, but they know it when they see it. In some cases, this ambiguity has led to abuse of the term and to a certain amount of cynicism surrounding it. At the same time, those who use it successfully to change schools or businesses are able to explain what it is and can describe the positive effects it has.

Based on my research in schools that have created a common focus for their collective efforts, I define vision as

> an agreement that is understood and shared by most staff in a school. It is a mixture of values, beliefs, purposes, and goals. It provides a clear reference point that staff use when making decisions about their own actions and the school's program. It is clear enough to enable staff to make the choices that help the school achieve the agreed-upon values, beliefs, purposes, or goals. It also allows progress and success to be judged more clearly.

Stated differently, a vision seems to provide an internal compass that helps people in large organizations understand more clearly how their actions relate to, or contribute to, the organization's goals. At its best, a vision provides, or restores, a sense of purpose and meaning to staff for whom such a sense has been lost or never existed.

This can be critically important in schools where educators lose sight of what they are trying to accomplish collectively because they are so isolated from one another individually. Without a vision, they make decisions based not on what the school needs to be doing for children, but on what makes the most sense to them based on their personal perspective on their students.

A school vision, and the associated processes of developing and renewing it, helps people reduce uncertainty, create common understanding, and find meaning in their day-to-day actions. Vision can be viewed as a way in which members of an organization attempt to create a broader sense of meaning and purpose for their actions. It can link people within the school who would otherwise have little in common other than the parking lot and lunch room.

Vision building in public schools is not easy. It requires time, which is often in short supply. It is frequently greeted with cynicism because it has the appearance of being the latest educational fad. It assumes that the people participating in the vision-building process initially share enough common beliefs and values to communicate and potentially agree on goals for the school. To be done correctly, it requires a great deal of preparation and work; extensive information about the school and trends in education and society generally must be collected and analyzed. And vision building can be very threatening, particularly if the vision that develops ends up favoring certain elements of the educational program over others.

Some general observations regarding prerequisites to successful vision building follow. Compare these to the characteristics of your own school to help determine the readiness and likely success of vision building.

1. A Previous History of and Success With Systematic School Improvement Efforts. Such a history seems to provide important conditions that encourage the leap of faith necessary to undertake vision building. In schools with a history of school improvement, staff often have a stronger sense of their ability to change the school, which leads them to see the value in creating a common direction. Previous experience with school improvement generally means that there are more teacher leaders, and more opportunities for teachers to develop skills such as communication and negotiation. These leaders and skills in turn help the vision-building process unfold successfully.

2. A Willingness to Examine Data in Various Forms and Employ Them in the Decision-Making Process. Data can take many forms, including

- Information about current practices at the school and the efficacy of those practices, such as attendance data

- Test results and other forms of assessment, including "exemplars" of student work demonstrating how well students do currently
- Reports from outside organizations, such as accrediting bodies
- State and district documents, including improvement plans, articulation plans, and curriculum frameworks
- Parent, teacher, or student surveys, including follow-up surveys of graduates and reports on performance of graduates in college
- Interviews with students, dropouts, transfers to private schools, members of the business community who hire graduates
- Observation of classroom practices at the school
- Journals and periodicals offering a perspective on current thinking and innovative practices in education, and on societal trends
- Information on the local, regional, or state economy, national outlook for job creation, international economic trends
- Visits to other school sites, or work sites, to learn firsthand about new techniques

All of this information feeds into the vision-building process to help overcome the tendency of educators to make decisions based primarily or solely on anecdotal or impressionistic information from the self-proclaimed faculty "expert" or from the person who is most emotional about an issue. Sometimes, these people have a valid point; but without data, there is no way to know if there is a problem, why there is a problem, and what solution most likely will solve the problem.

3. Principals Who Were Willing to Share Power and Decision Making to Some Degree. Some schools have "heroic" leaders with strong personal vision that they "sell" to the faculty through a variety of strategies. Some have leaders who simply create the conditions whereby faculty develop the vision.

It appears that both of these methods can work; however, the heroic principal must be ready to release personal ownership enough to allow the vision to become the staff's in order for it to take hold successfully. This may be difficult because when the vision becomes shared, it may change from what the principal envisioned initially. The willingness of principals with strong visions to step aside to some degree seems to be mandatory for successful vision building.

For those principals who do not express a personal vision, it seems necessary that they have some set of core beliefs about schooling. Therefore, even if they cannot define exactly what the vision ought to be, they know what they believe in and will prevent outcomes that are harmful to students. Vision building overseen by unprincipled individuals is an exercise in futility.

4. A Commitment to Act Upon the Results of the Vision-Building Process. In many schools that have already developed visions, no one is certain why the vision was created or to what purpose it has been put. These visions or missions often can be seen adorning school hallways, stationery, and business cards. This may be their major impact, because they seem to have little impact on school decisions or operations.

Faculty and community members are often reluctant to commit the time and energy necessary to develop a vision if they are not reasonably certain that the school will improve as a result of their efforts. Why should they sacrifice valuable time to create what seems like a vague statement of principle with little impact on them or the school?

When a vision is created successfully, staff already are aware of the role it will have after its creation. For example, they know that the vision will be used when programs are reviewed, budgets created, or new staff hired. When used in this way, the vision becomes an expression of the school's goals. Having a clearly identified role for the vision before the process begins raises the likelihood that the process will be successful and the vision will have the desired effect on the school.

5. A Central Office That Will Either Keep Out of the Process or Support It Actively. The central office is often viewed by people in schools as a hindrance to developing a vision. Although this perception is often accurate, it is worth testing before accepting as gospel. The central office may be more willing to allow schools to become clearly focused on improvement as authority is decentralized and accountability for improvement increases.

The most important role that central offices can play is to let schools know that they can proceed with the process of vision building without fear of reprisal. In addition, central office staff can provide

- A general districtwide vision, mission, and goals so that schools can compare their results to the district's and know they are in sync with district direction and goals
- Data not readily available to the sites that can help schools make decisions about not only their vision but also the goals they should adopt

- Assistance with the process in those instances where the people within central administration have the requisite technical skills

6. An Awareness That There Needs to Be Harmony Between the Vision and Goals of the School and Those of the District. Many districts have undertaken formal planning during the past several years. This process is often called strategic planning. In strategic planning, the district develops a vision, mission, goals, and strategies. These define a framework for district operations and school programs. The relationship between these centrally developed goals and individual school sites is often unclear. When schools develop visions, they must consider what the relationship is between what they create and what exists for the district as a whole. The school's vision and goals have to mesh in some critical ways with other schools in the district, because students generally attend more than one school as they progress.

In some districts, it may make sense for schools to have separate visions or missions that do not overlap. Some districts already have a wide range of magnet school programs, each having a specific theme or focus. However, even in this situation, there are certain basic beliefs about students and learning that should be held in common. A school's vision should strive to define a school uniquely while allowing it to work in a complementary fashion with the rest of a child's educational program.

Perhaps it would make sense in some districts for all schools to work together first to see what they believe in common before each site develops its vision. The results of this initial work then would be considered before any district-level planning process is undertaken. This "bottom-up, top-down" process might create greater ownership of both the school's and district's vision and mission.

The Challenge of Applying These Tools

Culture, commitment, and vision are powerful tools that help a school prepare for fundamental change. Unfortunately, there is no formula for applying them. Although many authors have offered detailed descriptions and guides for the change process, there are few true templates. Each school is unique; each requires careful analysis and a keen sense of the possible as restructuring is contemplated. For those educators, parents, community members, and students who are willing to accept the complexity of change, the tools described in this chapter can help galvanize and energize educational redesign in a school.

DISCUSSION QUESTIONS

1. Which elements of the school's culture serve to support restructuring?
2. Which elements of the culture might need to change for restructuring to occur?
3. Which of the Ten Commitments seem most challenging? Why? Which would make the most difference if agreed to by the faculty?
4. How do staff at the school determine their goals? How do goals affect their daily activities? How do they affect decisions made at the school? Do these goals reflect a vision or overall direction?
5. How are data used to shape goals and direction in the school?
6. Which of the prerequisites for successful vision building are present at the school? Which factors might hinder vision building?

12 Visions of a Restructured School

One of the real challenges of restructuring is how all the different things about schools that need to change can be combined into a coherent picture of how schooling might look at some point in the future. This chapter offers one view of how restructured schools may look and function differently. This description is designed, as is much of this book, primarily to provoke thought and discussion and to raise issues and possibilities for schools considering restructuring.

I do not think of this description as a set of goals that schools should necessarily pursue. Nor do I think that many schools will do most of the things contained in this description in the near future. At the same time, it reflects the fact that I believe the world has changed and that eventually schools will change as a result. I see most of these changes as inevitable; the question being more *when* than *whether.*

My concern is that if schools respond too slowly, they will become marginal institutions; they will no longer be at the center of communities, nor will they be the fabric that joins together and sustains the culture and society. The brief description that follows is an attempt to see how the pieces might fit together. So here are some of the ways in which I see schooling changing, along with some of the implications of those changes.

The purposes and goals of education will be questioned. Schools will ask the questions: What is an educated person? What will our graduates

140

look like and be able to do upon completion of their schooling? Clear statements of expected learning and skills will be stated as standards that provide an overall framework within which students will focus their efforts. The distinction between education as preparation of the mind and as preparation for work will lessen as the definition of an educated person and an effective worker begin to converge. Schools will strive to achieve two goals that have been separate in the past: They will have high standards, and they will ensure that essentially all students achieve the standards.

By establishing standards for student knowledge and performance and judging students and schools against these standards, much of what happens in schools will be revolutionized. The basic relationship between the student and the teacher will be transformed. Students will know what is expected of them and what they must do to demonstrate that they have reached required performance levels. Students will not seek to lower teacher expectations and requirements because students will be judged against standards that go beyond any one class or teacher; they will not benefit by spending time in a class that does not prepare them to meet standards. Teachers will truly need to be facilitators and coaches. Parents will compare their child's performance to published standards first and other children's standardized test scores second.

The line between curricular and extracurricular activities will disappear. It will not matter where students learned something, only that they can demonstrate that they meet required performance standards. Parents will be able to take more ownership for their child's learning. A wider variety of learning environments will be employed commonly in most schools, severely challenging traditional instructional methods. Data about how well students meet standards will be easily comparable across schools and much more useful than standardized achievement tests.

Performance levels above the required standard will allow students to continue to strive and achieve at higher levels than currently represented by an "A." The very existence of standards will allow more conversation about what students ought to know and what schools ought to teach. Curriculum will tend to be updated more regularly. Education will become a more flexible, adaptive process geared more closely to societal priorities and to student needs and capabilities.

The curriculum will be updated and adapted to reflect changes in society and in learners. Courses of study will be more integrated so that learners make connections among the different subjects they are taught and see the purposes and applications for what they are learning. The content that is taught will be scrutinized: Is it relevant, accurate, meaningful? Is there a compelling reason for children to know the material? What role should a textbook occupy in the curriculum? Are facts tools for understanding key concepts, or are they selected and taught arbitrarily? Must the material be organized in a fashion that guarantees fewer students master each succeeding level, or are there ways to move large numbers of students to higher levels of understanding? Can students move at their own pace where appropriate? Is the curriculum composed of things that everyone needs to know to function successfully in society and proceed successfully to higher levels of learning?

The world around the school will become a source for the curriculum. Local issues, problems, and resources will be integrated into the curriculum. Students in a mountain community in Colorado will learn about different things than will those in a rural school in Indiana, or an urban school in New York. Similar performance standards will be the thread that unites all of their learnings.

Real-world problems will be studied more frequently. Students in Oregon may study reforestation plans by analyzing them from geological, biological, ecological, economic, and political points of view. They may then present a report to the Forest Service and the county board of supervisors. Elementary schools may use the Internet to find help in identifying, researching, and posing solutions to a much wider variety of problems than exist in their local community. Kids will be able to make connections among the subjects they are learning, and between what they learn in school and how it applies to the world outside of school and to their lives.

The learner will move to the center of the instructional process. This will occur not by indulging the student, but by thinking of the student as a worker, a client, a partner, and an active participant. This will happen at least in part because it will be increasingly difficult to compel students to learn. Students will be called upon to put together the things they are learning, and to reach their own conclusions more often. Schools will not assume that students forget most of what they learn, and they will not reteach previously learned material as much. Learning will require more interaction between and among students, and between the student and a wider range of adults; there will be many opportunities for students to learn from one another. Students will demonstrate what they know publicly and will create strong norms of achievement within the school. They will come to support one another's learning and will understand that the only way to succeed is to achieve, not just put in the time. Teachers will be able to use a much wider variety of teaching techniques, particularly those that involve students actively.

Students will construct their own plans for learning. As they mature, they will accept greater amounts of responsibility for selecting learning experiences, organizing their time, and participating as a member of a team rather than being directed by a teacher. Their plans will personalize their education, but not individualize it. They will work within a broad framework of possible learning options and will learn, with the help of a wide range of adults, mentors, and peers, to take control of their learning, a skill that will ultimately result in their successful transition to lifelong learners.

Learning will have value and meaning to the learner. All learning will not be undertaken to prepare for work, but the connection between education and career will be much clearer. Many more experiences will be available to help students become aware of and explore career options. More students will give serious thought to what they want to become and will have opportunities to test out their dreams against the realities of the work world.

Students will learn to think in terms of quality as well as quantity. Worksheets, daily homework, fill-in-the-blank assignments, and other methods that occupy student time but produce low-quality work will be supplemented and replaced by an emphasis on quality. Students will have more opportunities to rework assignments, produce original pieces of work, and create products in which they have pride and ownership. They will come to understand what quality is. This understanding will be reflected in all their work. As a result, they will not only make things, but will take more pride in their writing and other, more traditional academic work. Teachers will learn how to shape and develop an understanding of quality by assessing work against quality standards and adopting the language and techniques of quality management.

The emphasis will be on success rather than sorting. It will not be acceptable for teachers to say, "I taught it; I've fulfilled my end of the bargain. It's up to them to learn it." Instructional methods will be examined and modified based on their actual success with children. Those techniques that consistently do not work with particular groups of students will not continue to be used with those students. Instructors will acknowledge the needs, capabilities, experiences, and unique challenges and motivations of the learner. This flexibility may lead to a substantial increase, not a decrease, in the amount of content that is taught at any given time to any given group of students.

The school will have many more ways of ensuring student success, and the culture of the school will have a deep and abiding belief that all students can and will learn at high levels. Failure will be considered to be a joint responsibility and a joint problem to be addressed in a partnership between student, parent, and school. In fact, many mechanisms will be available to help anticipate and head off student failure.

Assessment will be much more common, more public, and more complex. Schools will move beyond testing and evaluation to a wider variety of strategies geared to assess first and judge second. The purposes of assessment will be to provide students and parents with the information they need to continuously improve student performance, rather than simply to judge students after they complete a course of study.

Educators will use assessment to analyze larger and larger combinations of skills and abilities together. This will occur because teachers will have a curriculum that combines knowledge and skills across disciplines and that requires higher-level thinking from all students. Assessment will compare individual learner performance to clear, challenging standards. Sometimes, performance will be accomplished as a team member. Standardized measures that compare students only to one another regardless of overall quality will not be employed nearly as often.

Schools will strive to have all students meet high standards. When they do, it will not be a reason to believe that the curriculum is not challenging. In fact, consistently high performance will be cause for celebration. Assessment strategies that do not automatically divide students into winners and losers will displace methods such as standardized tests, where by definition no more than half the students are above average no matter how much they might actually know. Teachers will not have to devise artificial ways of spreading student grades to create a "normal" curve.

The ways and places in which learning occurs will be expanded dramatically. Many familiar ways of organizing students to learn will be modified, replaced, adapted, or enhanced. In both elementary and secondary schools, students may stay with the same teacher or group of teachers for more than one year. Students of varying ages will be taught in the same room. They will learn at their own pace and also serve as tutors for one another. They will move to the next level when their performance meets standards. Traditional forms of ability grouping, in particular, will be replaced by the use of more mixed-ability cooperative learning groups, cross-age grouping, peer tutors, and other strategies that emphasize success and continuous progress.

The idea that learning only occurs within a classroom under the control of a certified teacher will be replaced by models in which adults and children interact both within and outside the school building. Teachers with certificates will fill crucial roles as organizers, facilitators, diagnosticians, curriculum developers, assessors, and public relations experts. They will be assisted by highly skilled paraprofessionals, the educational equivalent of emergency medical technicians, who will be skilled at engaging students in learning tasks designed by supervising teachers. Other adults, young and old, will serve as mentors and role models through a much wider range of extracurricular activities.

Business people will visit schools more frequently and open up the work world (private sector, governmental, and nonprofit) to student exploration and participation. Community-based learning, service learning, apprenticeships, and internships will all enrich the educational options available to students. The community truly will be an extension of the school as students move in and out of the school, community, and workplace depending on the nature of their interests, studies, and the availability of learning experiences.

The boundary between high school and postsecondary learning in community colleges, 4-year colleges, and universities will blur. As students show that they are ready, learning experiences will be available, sometimes on-site, sometimes via technology, sometimes at a local college or university. More students will enter higher education with a clearer idea of what they wish to study, a better idea of the skills they need to succeed, and an improved probability that they will remain to receive a bachelor's degree.

Community colleges will link much more closely with high schools through "2 + 2" programs, where a student begins a course of study in high school that leads directly to 2 years of advanced training in the community college. Many more "professional-technical" options will be available to students, programs that do not require or lead to a 4-year degree but will prepare students for career-type jobs. High schools will do almost no specific job training, ceding this to community colleges or regional cooperative programs between high schools and community colleges. Community colleges will be a key link into local business communities and will offer many opportunities for students to explore the world of work.

There will be many more ways to structure time for learning than in short daily lessons or periods. Many different blocks of time will be created to allow teachers to organize learning in a variety of ways. This will allow more adults to spend time with fewer students. Students will have more opportunities to identify with adults and to make personal connections with the school. By increasing their affiliation with school, they will improve their performance.

The driving force for reorganizing time will be the need for students to meet standards and the need to assess their learning in relation to standards. Schools will have more seminars, workshops, intensive study sessions, labs, discussion groups, tutoring times, and other learning experiences of varying length. There will be periodic "assessment days" when more complicated assessments are conducted. Similarly, there may be "project days," "field experience days," or "community service days" where the entire student body devotes its efforts to a particular task or type of activity.

The length of the school day and school year will be reexamined. Schools will extend their programs—beginning earlier in the day, continuing into the evening, meeting on Saturdays, offering more summer opportunities. However, the programs available during these times will not necessarily be organized and staffed by teachers. Many of these activities will be offered by community agencies and others, including businesses, with interests in education. The times will correspond more to the needs of students and the community. The agricultural-based calendar gradually will be replaced with one geared to an information society.

The time available for learning will vary so that all students who want to can reach desired performance levels. The length of time each student spends in school will vary considerably based on his or her motivation, interests, and learning style. Because there will be numerous out-of-school learning opportunities, many students will meet required standards by spending most of their time in placements outside the school. Extended school year programs will provide more time for teachers to plan and develop new methods and materials and to organize and supervise a much wider range of learning experiences for students.

Technology will radically redefine the ways in which information is accessed and transmitted; it will not be a substitute for human interaction. In any emerging vision of education, technology has a transforming role. Although its uses are still being explored, its potential is clear.

Schools will no longer be the gateways to knowledge. Their libraries will not be the only or even the primary place that students go to obtain information. Teachers will need more than the content knowledge they carry in their heads to justify their positions.

Technology will be used to provide basic skills, interface with vast information sources outside the school, enable students to develop their creativity, manage information about student performance and achievement, organize and assist teachers in their quest to serve as instructor and clerk simultaneously, and serve as a tool through which students gain greater control over their own learning. Video will create more ways for students to learn and to demonstrate what they have learned.

More important, technology will create many opportunities for students to work together. Children who use technology in isolation at home will come to school to learn how to function socially and productively while continuing to develop and apply their technological skills.

Schools will become places where interesting questions or problems will be posed. Children will be guided in their exploration of timeless and current questions and issues. Technology will be a primary tool at every step. Computer labs will quickly become outmoded ways of providing students access to technology. There will be less teaching about technology and more use of it in a transparent fashion, so that student and teacher are barely conscious of the fact that they are using technology. Schools will be the place where technology is integrated into the human processes of learning, where it becomes an extension of the learner and the learning community. Schools will emphasize moral and ethical dilemmas; help students learn how to work together to solve problems; and make students aware of how information is accessed, ordered, and used. In short, they will be places where students learn how to transform information into knowledge.

School-community partnerships will be increasingly important to the success of every school. Parents will be true partners. They will help teachers develop learning programs for students, participate in the classroom on a more regular basis at all grade levels, make suggestions that assist professional educators, and take responsibility for creating an environment in the home that supports education.

The community at large will also play a new role in schools. Businesses and civic groups, local government, and social service agencies will all have a vital role to play by offering services; allowing workers to spend more time at school; serving as volunteers and tutors; providing advice, expertise, and resources; helping out at schools with extracurricular events or site beautification; taking on interns, apprentices, and observers; helping teachers develop new skills and knowledge; and generally accepting some responsibility for the education of the community's youth.

All of the services needed to help young people develop as healthy human beings will be more coordinated and integrated at the school. Community service agencies will provide services at the school in close coordination with teachers and administrators. Local government agencies will work more closely together to share resources, coordinate schedules, reduce overlap among agencies that serve youth, and perhaps even build new facilities jointly. More independent contractors and providers will contract with the school to offer services geared to the unique needs of particular students or groups of students. The goal will be to ensure that as many students as possible lead productive, socially responsible lives.

Decisions will be made with greater participation by those with an interest in education. Schools will function more as town halls in many important ways. They will be places where communities come together to consider important social, moral, and educational issues. The goals of the school will be discussed more openly, along with its effectiveness. As a result, schools will have stronger relations with the community and will be less subject to external pressure or interest groups. The role of administrators will be to help schools develop a vision and direction, to orchestrate the change process, to allocate resources in ways that help realize the vision, and to create new opportunities for teacher and community leadership to emerge. These administrators will see themselves not as the pinnacle of a pyramid, but as one point in a network that extends beyond the school itself and includes many people and organizations. Administrators will help direct the flow of energy throughout the network, rather than being the sole source of energy.

Teachers will continue to assume primary responsibility for determining the precise structure and content of the educational program. They will meet more regularly on substantive issues and have fewer meetings where they simply receive information or endorse decisions that have already been made. There will be a wider range of teacher leadership roles, including lead teachers, curriculum designers, assessment designers, assessment scorers, diagnosticians, staff developers, and community relations specialists. These teacher leaders will combine their classroom teaching duties with these specialist functions. Their skills as a teacher will not be lost to the school, but their role will be redefined to allow them to move in and out of their classrooms to provide specialized expertise to their colleagues.

These new teacher roles will stress collegiality and collaboration and will decrease teacher isolation. Teacher leaders will disseminate new ideas more rapidly and help create environments in which all teachers feel supported as they change their practices.

Site councils and other forms of participatory decision making will ensure regular, meaningful representation and participation by community members, parents, teachers, and students. These councils will not concern themselves with day-to-day issues, but will remain focused on more essential goals. They will gather and analyze information about student performance, ascertain the relevance and utility of the school's curriculum, set goals, suggest areas for teacher training and growth, promote new ideas and programs, and be positive forces for change and adaptation. These councils will be lively and unpredictable, comprising a range of perspectives beliefs, and personalities. Teachers will listen to and respect recommendations that originate in these councils. Principals will participate as equal voices with a unique responsibility to facilitate the council's success.

Schools will develop a stronger client orientation to cope with more competition. Schools will face challenges from private, charter, alternative, and home schooling. Each of these will be attractive to a particular clientele. However, rather than simply continuing to lose 5% of students here and 5% there to these service providers, schools will make a concerted effort to understand client needs better. They will redesign their programs based on these needs. This challenge will serve to reinvigorate and infuse new ideas into the system. Schools will become more adaptive. This adaptiveness will not be the solution to all educational problems, but will help speed the rate at which schools evolve.

One of the key motivators for these changes will be the realization by schools that each student lost costs the school thousands of dollars in state and local revenue. As budgets continue to tighten, schools will be more motivated to retain as many students as possible, including those whose needs often have been met outside the traditional school structure.

Schools will use adults in many new and different ways to help students develop and learn successfully. There will be a wider range of paid professionals in schools. In addition to changing the role of teachers, the role of the instructional assistant or aide will be expanded and reconceptualized with an eye toward creating a new category of educator who is truly a paraprofessional, not an aide. These individuals will work with small groups, provide supplementary instruction, and supervise students, thereby allowing the teacher to devote more time and energy to executive-level tasks, such as planning and diagnosing, addressing the needs of particularly difficult or demanding students, communicating with parents, developing curricula, and conducting and analyzing assessments.

The roles of other specialized personnel, such as counselors and special education and Chapter 1 teachers, will be reexamined to determine how their efforts can be best integrated and coordinated with the work of the classroom teacher. New teachers will be supervised more closely and given more assistance to ensure that every new teacher is excellent. Many more adult volunteers will help supplement the school's staff. Some will be paid hourly to teach a particular class; others will offer supplementary learning experiences that students pay for on a sliding scale.

Traditional relationships between teachers' unions, administrators, and boards of education will become more collaborative to solve problems and improve schools. Labor relations in school districts will still be governed by contracts, but these contracts will be broad frameworks within which individual schools can pursue improvement. Wages and benefits will be the key elements of these contracts, but educational practices will be left to schools to a much greater degree. Waivers will be granted to individual schools when needed, and more problems will be addressed outside the contract and away from the bargaining table. Although teachers' unions will continue to be important, they will begin to function more as partners and operate more as professional associations than as trade unions. Mechanisms such as joint committees of teachers, administrators, and board members will explore solutions to problems as they arise rather than allowing everything to build up to negotiations. Collaborative bargaining strategies will seek to build trust among all participants.

How Realistic Is This Vision?

Rarely, if ever, will all the elements in this vision be present in any one school or district. Most ongoing attempts to redesign schooling will be able to include only a subset of these elements. Taken as a whole, the general description I offer here provides a picture in broad brush strokes of the ways in which many educators, policymakers, and others who write about schooling are thinking about how education might transform itself.

This vision suggests ways that education can help the entire community and the economic system. It tends to reflect the increased emphasis on each student as an individual. It assumes that teachers will have more content knowledge, more teaching techniques, heightened professionalism, greater sophistication, and enhanced leadership skills. The vision acknowledges the need for new partnerships to emerge for education to succeed in a complex, global information society. And it suggests fundamental overhaul of curriculum, instruction, and assessment as the starting point and continuing focal point of all educational change.

This vision of education contains many elements that have been suggested before at one time or another. Is all of this simply a rehashing of earlier reform movements? Yes, in the sense that there really is very little in education that has not been tried before; no, in the sense that many of these elements fit the needs of schools and society today better than when they were initially proposed or attempted. The context in which these ideas are being applied now is fundamentally different from what existed the last time they were attempted. Current problems and societal trends now demand many changes that might have been attempted with less success at a previous time.

It's very difficult to bring about significant change in schools. I acknowledge the difficulties that schools face when they attempt to change. I say this not to discourage those considering or involved in large-scale change in their schools, but to be candid about how changes that challenge people's assumptions can be disruptive and draining.

Part of readiness is knowing that you are prepared for what lies ahead—that you are ready to give up some of the peace and tranquility in your life and become engulfed in conflict, anxiety, uncertainty, and discomfort. Is it worth it? Each person answers this question differently. Some people thrive on chaos; others abhor it. It is worth sizing up your own attitude about change and your own personal comfort level with conflict before embarking on the journey that is transformational school reform.

I offer this vision not because it should be anyone's blueprint or ultimate goal, but to suggest both the distance that there is to travel and the possibilities for improvement and transformation that the journey offers. My purpose in this book is not to outline how to make the journey, but to encourage those who are considering restructuring to ask themselves the one basic question posed throughout the book: Are you ready to restructure? Hopefully, as you read and discussed this book, you moved closer to an answer to the question. If you decided that you are ready, you have taken the first and in some ways the most difficult step down the road to fundamental educational restructuring and improvement.

RESOURCE A

List of Organizations
Concerned With Restructuring

Education Reform Resource Organizations List

This resource list is divided into two sections. Groups in the first section address education reform policy issues, including coordination; groups in the second section emphasize restructuring at the local level.

I. Systemwide Policy Issues

Annenberg Institute for School Reform, Brown University, Box 1969, Providence, RI 02912, (401) 863-7990

Directed by Theodore Sizer, chair of the Coalition of Essential Schools, this new institute will promote the idea that all students should be expected to perform up to rigorous academic standards. It will issue an annual progress report on school reform and provide seminars, telecommunications products, and publications. The institute will form alliances with educators and kindred reform organizations. It will also track the progress of various reform initiatives and develop critiques, designs, and examples to accelerate these initiatives.

NOTE: This list is reprinted from ERIC Digest (Fall, 1994), Vol. 3, Issue 2, pp. 18-21.

Center for Education Reform, 1001 Connecticut Avenue NW, Suite 920, Washington, DC 20036, (202) 822-9000

This clearinghouse provides information on school choice, accountability, and general education reform. It maintains a database; publishes summary papers on school choice, charter schools, standards, and testing; and supports coalition-building efforts for school choice on the state and district levels.

Center for Leadership in School Reform (CLSR), 950 Breckenridge Lane, Suite 200, Louisville, KY 40207, (502) 895-1942

This nonprofit center, founded in 1988 by Phillip Schlechty, works to support systemic restructuring by developing partnerships with school districts to assist them in developing their capacity to support and sustain building-level change. CLSR advocates creating conditions in which schools are organized around students and the work they are expected to do, and, in addition, communities are organized to guarantee each child the support needed to be successful in school and in the community.

Center for Systemic School Reform (CSSR), San Francisco State University, 221 Burk Hall, 1600 Holloway Avenue, San Francisco, CA 94132, (415) 338-3059

This new organization, directed by Bill Honig, former state superintendent of California, will provide a link between public schools; state reform efforts; and reform networks focused on student performance and comprehensive, long-term changes in areas such as instruction, organization, assessment, accountability, team building, staff development, parent involvement methodologies, and the treatment of at-risk youngsters. CSSR has set three initial goals: (a) to identify and develop techniques to assist large numbers of schools in changing their instructional programs to meet new content and performance standards; (b) to train a core group of professionals to help public schools become world class; and (c) to refine the technology of assistance by providing full-service technical support to 250 public schools committed to becoming self-sustained, world-class institutions. CSSR will conduct research, hold conferences and seminars, interact with school reform leaders, and develop a resource center on successful reform programs and model curricula. Educators and administrators who would like to contribute papers, model curricula, or other information they have gained in their school reform efforts should send material to CSSR.

Center on Organization and Restructuring of Schools, University of Wisconsin, 1025 West Johnson Street, Madison, WI 53706, (608) 263-7575

The Center on Organization and Restructuring of Schools, a research center funded by the U.S. Department of Education's Office of Educational Research and Improvement, studies how the organizational features of schools can be changed to increase the intellectual and social competence of students. The center's research and analysis is focused on restructuring in four areas: the experiences of students in school; the professional life of teachers; the governance, management, and leadership of schools; and the coordination of community resources to better serve educationally disadvantaged students. To be placed on the center's mailing list, contact Karen Prager, Dissemination Coordinator.

Consortium for Policy Research in Education (CPRE), Carriage House at the Eagleton Institute of Politics, Rutgers University, 86 Clifton Avenue, New Brunswick, NJ 08901-1568, (908) 932-1331

CPRE, a research center funded by the U.S. Department of Education's Office of Educational Research and Improvement, unites researchers from Rutgers, Harvard, Stanford, the University of Michigan, and the University of Wisconsin at Madison to improve student learning through research on education policy and finance. CPRE examines state and local policies that promote high levels of learning for students from diverse social and economic backgrounds and that lead to greater coherence between state and local actions.

Education Reform Resource Organizations List Council of Chief State School Officers (CCSSO), One Massachusetts Avenue NW, Suite 700, Washington, DC 20001-1431, (202) 408-5505

The council sponsors the State Leadership Project, in which information is compiled and exchanged on what the states are doing to pursue comprehensive changes in areas such as student learning, assessment, teacher training, finance, and governance. CCSSO is also helping states to reorganize their education departments in preparation for developing and implementing systemic reform plans under the GOALS 2000: Educate America Act.

Education Commission of the States (ECS), 707 17th Street, Suite 2700, Denver, CO 80202-3427, (303) 299-3600

ECS is a nationwide, interstate compact formed in 1965 to help governors, state legislators, state education officials, and others develop policies to improve education at all levels. ECS conducts policy research, maintains an information clearinghouse, organizes forums, and provides technical assistance to leaders in 53 member states and territories. It supports systemic reform, which ECS defines as "the alignment of policy, practice, and people's roles and responsibilities within the education system and other interrelated systems to achieve a new vision of teaching and learning for all children."

ERIC Clearinghouse on Educational Management, University of Oregon, 1787 Agate Street, Eugene, OR 97403-5207, (800) 438-8841

This clearinghouse, one of 16 sponsored by the U.S. Department of Education's ERIC program, abstracts and indexes journal articles and documents covering the leadership, management, and structure of public and private education organizations; school administrators and administration; organizational change; and education facilities management. The clearinghouse also prepares research syntheses, bibliographies, literature reviews, monographs, and books in these subject areas and maintains a listserv on the Internet for K-12 administrators.

Institute for Educational Leadership (IEL), 1001 Connecticut Avenue NW, Suite 310, Washington, DC 20036, (202) 822-8405

IEL is a nonprofit corporation that promotes the free exchange of ideas on complex issues to assist education professionals in making informed decisions and policies. It conducts impartial forums to link and inform education policymakers and operates programs to develop education leadership. IEL also offers access to policy analysis and expertise on critical education issues.

National Alliance for Restructuring Education, 700 Eleventh Street NW, Suite 750, Washington, DC 20005, (202) 783-3668

This project of the National Center for Education and the Economy supports partnerships involving states, school districts, foundations, corporations, and nonprofit organizations committed to systemic change to improve learning for all children. The alliance provides funding, training, and technical assistance in five areas: standards and assessment, learning environments, community services and support, high performance management, and public engagement.

National Center on Educational Outcomes for Students With Disabilities, University of Minnesota, 350 Elliott Hall, 75 East River Road, Minneapolis, MN 55455, (612) 626-1530

This research center sponsored by the U.S. Department of Education's Office of Special Education and Rehabilitative Services collects and evaluates information on how state assessments and national standards affect students with disabilities and studies how alternative testing accommodations and adaptations can be made for these students. The center also works to build consensus among state directors, educators, and parents on which education outcomes are of importance to all students.

National Conference of State Legislatures (NCSL), 1560 Broadway, Suite 700, Denver, CO 80202, (303) 830-2200

This organization for state legislators and legislative staff provides research, training, development, and publications on a variety of policy areas, including education. NCSL helps policymakers keep up with education program developments in other states through meetings and publications such as *Reinventing Education* ($15), a new title in the Investing in People series.

National Education Goals Panel, 1850 M Street NW, Suite 270, Washington, DC 20036, (202) 632-0952

The National Education Goals Panel, a bipartisan group of state governors, members of Congress, and administration officials, was created in 1990 and codified in the GOALS 2000: Educate America Act to build public support for the goals and to monitor the nation's progress. The National Education Goals Panel will also review voluntary standards submitted to the National Education Standards and Improvement Council. The panel prepares annual reports that summarize state and national statistical data related to each of the goals.

National Governors' Association (NGA), 444 North Capitol Street, Suite 267, Washington, DC 20001-1512, (202) 624-5320

NGA operates a Restructuring Schools Project to help states redesign their school systems by rethinking the role of teachers and administrators, changing account-ability systems, and sponsoring or encouraging innovation. NGA's Education Policy Studies staff work closely with other education, political, and business groups, as well as policymakers, in every state to study education reform. NGA offers publi-cations, conferences, and technical assistance to help states implement education reforms.

National Science Foundation (NSF), Office of Systemic Reform, 4201 Wilson Boulevard, Arlington, VA 22230, (703) 306-1690

NSF sponsors the State Systemic Initiatives program, which promotes higher achievement in science, mathematics, engineering, and technology education through changes in the state education system in areas such as curricula, materials, technology, assessment, teacher preparation, and decision making. NSF also funds urban and rural systemic initiatives to coordinate efforts to improve science and mathematics education in elementary and secondary schools. The urban program focuses on K-12 education in the 25 American cities with the highest concentrations of low-income children; it provides assistance for changing policies, practices, and procedures over a 5-year period. The rural systemic initiatives program funds regional projects to remove barriers to systemic and sustainable improvements in science, mathematics, and technology education in 20 low-income, rural areas.

New Standards Project, 700 11th Street NW, Suite 750, Washington, DC 20001, (202) 783-3668

The New Standards Project is a joint program of the National Center on Education and the Economy in Rochester, New York, and the Learning Research and Development Center at the University of Pittsburgh. A group of states and local school districts that were designing and administering performance-based assessments have become partners in this effort to produce performance- and portfolio-based assessments linked with high national standards. The partners include the states of Arkansas, California, Colorado, Connecticut, Delaware, Florida, Iowa, Kentucky, Maine, Massachusetts, Missouri, New York, Oregon, Pennsylvania, South Carolina, Texas, Vermont, Virginia, and Washington and the school districts in Fort Worth, New York City, Pittsburgh, Rochester, San Diego, and White Plains.

Re:Learning, Education Commission of the States, 707 17th Street, Suite 2700, Denver, CO 80202-3427, (303) 299-3600

This partnership between the Education Commission of the States and the Coalition for Essential Schools is designed to improve student learning by re-designing states' education systems "from the schoolhouse to the statehouse." Re:Learning does not promote a specific model; instead, it provides a set of principles and processes for considering school and state reform. Participating schools agree to adopt the nine "Common Principles" developed by the Coalition of Essential Schools, whereas district and state leaders work on changes in admin-istration, governance, and policy to stimulate and support school innovation.

II. School Restructuring Networks

Accelerated Schools Project, Stanford University, CERAS Building, Stanford, CA 94305-3084, (415) 725-1676

This project, developed by Henry Levin and colleagues at the Center for Education Research at Stanford, emphasizes the improvement of the academic performance of disadvantaged students by acceleration rather than remediation. It proposes to eliminate achievement gaps by changing curriculum, instruction, and school organization. The Accelerated Schools Project was piloted in elementary schools in California in 1986 and is now in operation in California, Connecticut, Illinois, Missouri, and other states.

Coalition of Essential Schools, Brown University, Box 1969, Providence, RI 02912, (401) 863-3384

Founded by Theodore Sizer in 1984, the Coalition of Essential Schools supports secondary schools, districts, and states in their efforts to focus on schools' primary purpose: to improve student learning. The coalition asks practitioners to work from a set of ideas—the nine "Common Principles"—to restructure their own schools based on the particular needs of their community. It publishes a newsletter, *Horace,* that covers activities under way at coalition schools.

League of Schools Reaching Out, Boston University, 605 Commonwealth Avenue, Boston, MA 02215 (617) 353-3309

The League of Schools Reaching Out is a project of the Institute for Responsive Education (IRE), a nonprofit, public-interest organization that promotes parent and citizen involvement in education with a special emphasis on equity issues. It is an international network of approximately 90 schools with partnerships involving families and communities. IRE provides some schools with facilitators to help coordinate three key project components: a parent center, parent outreach workers, and teacher researcher teams.

National Center for Restructuring Education, Schools, and Teaching, Teachers College, Columbia University, Box 110, New York, NY 10027, (212) 678-3434

This membership organization is intended to connect individuals and organizations working to build learner-centered schools. It offers publications, conferences, workshops, and technical assistance. Linda Darling-Hammond and Ann Lieberman are the codirectors. Write or call for membership information and a publications list.

National Diffusion Network (NDN), U.S. Department of Education, 555 New Jersey Avenue NW, Washington, DC 20208-5645, (202) 219-2134

Supported by the U.S. Department of Education's Office of Educational Research and Improvement, the National Diffusion Network helps to inform educators about highly effective education programs from other schools and districts. These programs are validated or examined for proof of effectiveness by a Program Effectiveness Panel. Program information is compiled in annual editions of a catalog called Educational Programs That Work. Facilitators are available in every state, the District of Columbia, and the U.S. territories to help local school districts identify programs that meet their needs and obtain the assistance needed to implement these programs successfully. Developers of successful programs are available to train teachers in the adopting schools.

National Network for Educational Renewal, University of Washington College of Education, 313 Miller Hall, Mailstop DQ 12, Seattle, WA 98195, (206) 543-6162

This network is composed of school-university partnerships committed to the simultaneous renewal of schooling and the education of educators. John Goodlad's Center for Educational Renewal serves as the hub of the network. Approximately 25 colleges and universities, 100 school districts, and 250 partner schools in 14 states are linked to the National Network for Educational Renewal. The network emphasizes forming partnerships, strengthening liberal arts and professional curricula, and developing a system of rewards and incentives for faculty members.

New American Schools Development Corporation (NASDC), 1000 Wilson Boulevard, Suite 2710, Arlington, VA 22209, (703) 908-9500

NASDC, a private, bipartisan, nonprofit organization headed by David Kearns, former Deputy Secretary of Education, was founded in 1991 by corporate and foundation leaders to support the design and creation of outstanding public schools. NASDC selected 11 design and development teams from a pool of nearly 700 proposals and now supports 9 teams in the implementation of their designs. Teams include ATLAS Communities, Audrey Cohen College, Community Learning Centers, Co-NECT Schools, Expeditionary Learning/Outward Bound, Los Angeles Learning Centers, Modern Red Schoolhouse, National Alliance for Restructuring Education, and Roots and Wings. The teams currently work with 140 schools in 19 states. Following refinement of their designs, they will aid other interested communities in adapting and implementing their prototypes for school reform. Contact NASDC for a brochure on the design teams.

School Development Program, Yale Child Study Center, 230 South Frontage Road, P.O. Box 3333, New Haven, CT 06510

This program, founded in 1968 by James Comer, is designed to improve the academic performance and school success of low-income minority students by building supportive bonds among children, parents, and school staff, thereby promoting a positive school climate. The Comer process emphasizes a no-fault atmosphere, collaborative working relationships, and decision making by consensus. Each school in this program establishes the following teams: a school planning and management team that includes parents, teachers, administrators, and support staff; a mental health team that addresses children's developmental needs; and a parents' group that strengthens the bond between home and school.

Success for All, Center for Social Organization of Schools, Johns Hopkins University, 3505 North Charles Street, Baltimore, MD 21218, (410) 516-0370

This program of the Center for Research on Effective Schooling for Disadvantaged Students emphasizes the restructuring of elementary schools and the reconfiguring of the uses of Chapter 1 and special education funds to emphasize prevention and early intervention rather than remediation. Under the direction of Robert Slavin, Success for All has expanded beyond Baltimore to about 85 schools in 19 states. Its principal features include reading tutors, direct instruction, and flexible grouping in reading; frequent assessment; enriched preschool and kindergarten programs; and family support teams.

RESOURCE B

Next Steps in Restructuring:
Questions to Ask

This resource is a series of questions keyed to twelve dimensions of restructuring that are designed to enable a faculty to determine focal points for programs of school restructuring.

	Yes, consistently	Generally	Inconsistently	Infrequently	No	Priority
Performance standards						
1. Are learning standards specified? Do they form the basis for assessment?						
2. Are the standards consistent with the vision and goals of the school?						
3. Were the school's standards developed with broad community involvement and with reference to the skills students need to succeed in the future?						
4. Are the standards a combination of intellectual processes, skills, and content knowledge that provides a clear framework within which assessment can occur?						
5. Are the standards clear to teachers, students, and parents?						
6. Are the expected learning performances cumulative throughout a child's education—kindergarten through graduation? Are there benchmarks that suggest the acceptable range of performance at various ages?						

	Yes, consistently	Generally	Inconsistently	Infrequently	No	Priority
Curriculum						
1. To what degree is the content knowledge contained in all courses accurate and up-to-date?						
2. Does the curriculum prepare learners for the future?						
3. Does the curriculum consciously balance between basic factual knowledge and higher-level concepts?						
4. Is the required course of study consistent with the school's vision?						
5. Is the curriculum designed to build outward from students' life experiences and learning opportunities that surround the school?						
6. Do different social/ethnic/economic groups learn substantially different content?						
Instruction						
1. Are students active participants in classroom activities and in choosing how they learn?						
2. Are individualized learner goals developed?						
3. Is factual information used as a foundation for developing higher level concepts rather than as an end in itself?						
4. Do the learning tasks cause the learner to integrate information and concepts across disciplines?						
5. Do real-world problems serve to focus and apply lessons and material taught?						
6. Is instruction designed so that all students can potentially succeed?						
7. Do members of different social/ethnic/economic groups work together cooperatively to solve problems and apply knowledge?						
Assessment						
1. Are curriculum instruction and assessment clearly and consciously linked in the school's total instructional program?						
2. Are a variety of assessment methods used appropriately to develop a complex and accurate portrait of student performance and knowledge?						
3. Does assessment include public demonstrations by students?						
4. Do students assess themselves at any point?						
5. Does assessment provide formative as well as summative data to students, parents, and teachers?						
6. Does assessment involve the application of information to solve real-world problems?						
7. Do students have any choices about how they are assessed?						
8. Do members of different social/ethnic/economic groups perform differently on particular assessments?						
Technology						
1. Is technology used both to transmit factual information in a structured manner and to empower learners to explore and discover?						
2. Are teachers mastering and using technology personally?						
3. Is technology viewed broadly to include applications in addition to computers?						
4. Is appropriate software purchased along with hardware?						

	Yes, consistently	Generally	Inconsistently	Infrequently	No	Priority
5. Is appropriate training made available when hardware is purchased?						
6. Are curriculum content and instructional techniques changing in tandem with new technology acquisitions?						
Time						
1. Is time being adapted to learning needs rather than vice versa?						
2. Is time structured to respond to needs and realities of students' and parents' lives?						
3. Are staff and curriculum development preceding and accompanying changes in time?						
4. Is extra time being provided to those students who need it to reach desired or required performance levels?						
5. Are the boundaries of time being reconceptualized beyond traditional limits of 7 a.m. to 3 p.m., 5 days per week, 180 days per year?						
Learning environment						
1. Is the learning environment being designed with the needs and realities of the learner in mind?						
2. Is the learning environment perceived as extending beyond the classroom? The school? The community?						
3. Are grouping practices being reexamined to determine their effect on children from different social/ethnic/economic groups as well as their effect on the school culture and climate?						
4. Is the learning environment being designed to maximize positive interpersonal relationships among students and between students and adults?						
5. Are curriculum, instruction, and assessment changing in ways that support and take advantage of any changes in the learning environment?						
School-community relations						
1. Are parents being included as partners in the establishment of goals for their own children?						
2. Are parents provided enough information of the right sort to participate as partners in the education of their children and the running of the school?						
3. Are the needs of parents considered in the organization of the school and in the expectations held for parents?						
4. Is the broader community invited to participate in specific ways?						
5. Are there specific ways that parents and community members can be involved in key decisions regarding the school?						
6. Is the community involved in and informed about changes in the school?						
Governance						
1. Is decision making participatory?						
2. Are decisions made in relation to a vision?						
3. Are existing decision-making structures modified and new structures added as necessary?						
4. Is decision making open and inclusive?						
5. Are changes in governance viewed as means to ends, not as ends in themselves?						

	Yes, consistently	Generally	Inconsistently	Infrequently	No	Priority
Teacher leadership						
1. Are a range of opportunities for teacher leadership being provided?						
2. Is training in leadership and group process provided when teachers need it?						
3. Do teacher leaders retain connections to the classroom?						
4. Does the culture of the school support teachers emerging as leaders and taking leadership roles?						
5. Is there evidence over time of continuous growth in the ability of teachers to lead?						
6. Do teachers have the opportunity to develop a broader perspective on their classroom and school via readings, visitations, conferences, discussions, and so on?						
7. Are leadership opportunities offered to a wide range of teachers?						
Personnel						
1. Are people other than certified teachers becoming involved in teaching or in supporting the instructional process?						
2. Is there an emphasis on excellence in the teaching staff, with no acceptance of mediocrity or tolerance of incompetence?						
3. Do the teachers want to be where they are? Are they excited about teaching, and do they truly care about young people?						
4. Are the current distribution and allocation of staff within the school consistent with the school's vision and mission?						
Working relationships						
1. Are there efforts to include the professional association as a partner in change?						
2. Is there exploration at the district level of alternative forms of bargaining?						
3. Is there agreement to leave much of the restructuring program out of the negotiated agreement, subject to specified guidelines?						
4. Are there good-faith efforts to redefine the role of the professional association in a positive way?						

RESOURCE C

Annotated Bibliography

Education Reform Reading List

The following titles cover a range of issues related to education reform, particularly at the systemwide level. Ordering information is included at the end of each entry. In addition, publications with an ED number have been abstracted and are included in the ERIC database. You may read them on microfiche at more than 3,000 locations worldwide or order microfiche or paper copies from the ERIC Document Reproduction Service at 1-800-443-ERIC (3742). For details, contact ACCESS ERIC at 1-800-LET-ERIC (538-3742).

"The Best Path to Systemic Educational Policy: Standard/Centralized or Differentiated/Decentralized?" William H. Clune, Fall 1993

This article in *Educational Evaluation and Policy Analysis* (Volume 15, Number 3, pp. 233-254) provides an alternative view of a centralized strategy of mandatory curriculum frameworks, high-stakes student assessments, and coordinated teacher training. The author proposes instead a "practical, change-oriented system built from the bottom up" involving local choice of curricula consistent with the various curriculum networks, as well as capacity building through technical assistance and professional development. Check your library or order a reprint from University Microfilms International, 300 North Zeeb Road, Ann Arbor, MI 48106-1346; (800) 521-0600, extension 2786.

NOTE: This bibliography is reprinted from ERIC Digest, Vol. 3, Issue 2, Fall, 1994, pp. 22-25.

"Beyond Common Sense in Educational Restructuring: The Issues of Content and Linkage," Fred M. Newmann, March 1993

This article in *Educational Researcher* (Volume 22, Number 2, pp. 4-13, 22) describes an agenda of content for teacher commitment and competence based on such factors as depth of understanding, success for all students, new teacher roles, and the concept of schools as moral communities. Problems related to organizational change, standards, local empowerment, funding, and social capital are addressed. Check your library or order a reprint from University Microfilms International, 300 North Zeeb Road, Ann Arbor, MI 48106-1346; (800) 521-0600, extension 2786.

Bringing Coherence to State Policy: Restructuring the Education System, **Education Commission of the States, 1992, ED 350 675**

This report (SI-92-4) suggests that the key to major improvement of the education system lies in redefining the policy area that should drive reform in a given state and linking other policy areas to that effort. It outlines and gives examples of state progress in the areas of standards and curriculum, assessment and accountability, governance, professional development, higher education, finance, cross-agency collaboration, and diversity/choice options. $4 plus $2.50 postage and handling; discount for bulk quantities. Education Commission of the States, 707 17th Street, Suite 2700, Denver, CO 80202-3427; (303) 299-3600.

Designing Coherent Education Policy: Improving the System, **Susan H. Fuhrman, ed., 1993; ED 359 626**

This 310-page book provides an in-depth look at systemic school reform and offers ideas on how educators at the district, state, and federal levels can coordinate the various elements of policy infrastructure around a new set of ambitious, common goals for student achievement. $32.95. Jossey-Bass Publishers, 350 Sansome Street, San Francisco, CA 94104; (415) 433-1767.

Educational Programs That Work, **National Diffusion Network, 1993**

This annual catalog describes nearly 200 exemplary education programs on the elementary, secondary, and higher education levels. These programs have been validated by a Program Effectiveness Panel affiliated with the U.S. Department of Education's National Diffusion Network (NDN). Validation is based on convincing evidence that the programs caused academic gains superior to those from standard school procedures. Each edition includes contact information for state NDN facilitators. $11.95, plus $3.00 shipping and handling for first copy; add $1.00 for each additional copy. Sopris West Incorporated, 1140 Boston Avenue, Longmont, CO 80501; (303) 651-2829.

From Risk to Renewal, **Editors of Education Week, 1993**

This 300-page paperback addresses the major questions that confront U.S. educators and policymakers in the areas of school reorganization, student standards, accountability, teacher development, school finance, and education change. $12.95 per copy; discount for bulk quantities. Editorial Projects in Education, Inc., 4301 Connecticut Avenue NW, Suite 432, Washington, DC 20008; (202) 686-0800.

The Governance of Curriculum, **Richard F. Elmore and Susan H. Fuhrman, eds., 1994**

In this yearbook, 11 scholars address federal, state, and district roles in the development and implementation of standards and curriculum. The three-part book covers national and state policy development, state curriculum reforrns, and district and school roles in reform. $19.95 plus $2.50 postage and handling. Association for Supervision and Curriculum Development, 1250 North Pitt Street, Alexandria, VA 22314-1403; (703) 549-9110.

Introduction to Systemic Education Reform: Restructuring the Education System, **Education Commission of the States, 1992, ED 350 677**

This bulletin (SI-92-1) describes the coherent policy environment necessary for comprehensive education reform to occur and suggests policies for states to support in the areas of new academic standards, curriculum and assessment alignment, professional development, accountability, and interagency cooperation. $3.00, plus $2.50 postage and handling; quantity discounts. Education Commission of the States, 707 17th Street, Suite 2700, Denver, CO 80202-3427; (303) 299-3600.

Issues and Strategies in Systemic Reform, **Susan H. Fuhrman and Diane Massell, 1992, ED 356 528**

This paper highlights issues and strategies associated with systemic reform, which pairs ambitious, coordinated state policies with professional discretion at the school site. It covers such topics as building political support for systemic reform, involving the public and school personnel in reform, and examining the equity implications and financing of systemic reform strategies. $10.00. Consortium for Policy Research in Education, Carriage House at the Eagleton Institute of Politics, Rutgers University, 86 Clifton Avenue, New Brunswick, NJ 08901-1568; (908) 932-1331.

Overcoming Barriers to Educational Restructuring: A Candor System Literacy, **Grady McGonagill, 1993, ED 357 512**

This paper (Stock No. 21 00397) promotes "system literacy," or a deep under- standing of how organizations function, as a useful approach to creating support strategies for restructuring. Without system literacy, systemic reform may lack a sense of urgency in school systems, in addition to lacking a strong partnership of support, a strategic direction, and innovative methods. $2.50, plus $3.50 shipping and handling; bulk rates available. American Association of School Administrators, 1801 North Moore Street, Arlington, VA 22209; (703) 875-0730.

Putting the Pieces Together: Systemic School Reform, **Consortium for Policy Research in Education, 1991, ED 343 215**

This policy brief summarizes Marshall S. Smith's and Jennifer O'Day's analytic essay, "Systemic School Reform," which discusses research on the effectiveness of current education policies and policy system development in a number of states. The essay proposes a strategy for systemic reform that would combine both top-down and bottom-up approaches and feature a unifying vision and goals, coherent instructional guidance, and restructured governance. Free. Consortium for Policy Research in Education, Carriage House at the Eagleton Institute of Politics, Rutgers University, 86 Clifton Avenue, New Brunswick, NJ 08901-1568; (908) 932-1331.

Reinventing Our Schools, **Phi Delta Kappa and the Association for Instructional Technology, 1993**

This staff development videotape provides six 30-minute interviews with the following education reform leaders: James Comer, MD, professor of child psychiatry at the Yale Child Study Center; Linda Darling-Hammond, professor at the Columbia University Teachers College and codirector of the National Center for Restructuring Education Schools, and Teaching; Howard Gardner, director of Project Zero at the Harvard Graduate School of Education; Ann Lieberman, professor at the Columbia University Teachers College and codirector of the National Center for Restructuring Education, Schools, and Teaching; Phillip Schlechty, president of the Center for Leadership in School Reform; and Ted Sizer, chairman of the Brown University Department of Education and founder of the Coalition of Essential Schools. $495 plus $10 processing. Center for Professional Development, Phi Delta Kappa, P.O. Box 789, Bloomington, IN 47402-0789; (800) 766-1156.

Roadmap to Restructuring, **David T. Conley, 1993, ED 359 593**

This 432-page handbook provides a synthesis of research and practical knowledge on change and transformation in schools. It covers the historical background of and reasons for education restructuring; the roles of federal and state governments, school districts, parents, and the community; 12 dimensions of restructuring, ranging from curriculum and learner outcomes to personnel issues and school governance; and the process of restructuring. $19.95. ERIC Clearinghouse on Educational Management, University of Oregon, 1787 Agate Street, Eugene, OR 97403-5207; (800) 438-8841.

School Change Models and Processes: A Review and Synthesis of Research and Practice, **Marshall Sashkin and John Egermeier, 1993, ED 351 757**

This booklet describes three dominant perspectives on education change: the rational-scientific perspective, which posits that change is created by disseminating innovative techniques; the political or "top-down" perspective, in which change is generated from legislation and other external directives; and the cultural or "bottom-up" perspective that creates change by encouraging value changes within organizations. It investigates strategies used for school change, including fixing the parts (curricula, teaching methods), fixing the people, fixing the schools, and fixing the system. Single copies free. Education Information Branch, Office of Educational Research and Improvement, 555 New Jersey Avenue NW, Washington, DC 20208-5720; (800) 424-1616.

Schools of Thought: How the Politics of Literacy Shape Thinking in the Classroom, **Rexford G. Brown, 1991, ED 331 151**

This book is focused on the new, higher literacy, which goes beyond the requirements of a high school diploma and includes capacities once demanded only of a collegebound elite. Chapters discuss a "literacy of thoughtfulness" in relation to education in rural America and the South, on an Indian reservation, in an urban school district, and at state and district policy levels. $24.95. Jossey-Bass Publishers, 350 Sansome Street, San Francisco, CA 94104; (415) 433-1767

Standard Setting as Educational Reform: Trends and Issues Paper No. 8, **Gary Sykes and Peter Plastrik, 1993; ED 358 068**

This paper examines the role of standard setting in three models of education reform: the systemic reform model, the professional model, and the reform network model. It was prepared to stimulate discussion within the National Council for Accreditation of Teacher Education (NCATE) community, states, and other reform agencies. $17.50. ERIC Clearinghouse on Teaching and Teacher Education, One Dupont Circle NW, Suite 610, Washington, DC 20036-1186; (800) 822-9229.

The State's Role in Effecting Systemic Change: A Northwest Depiction, **Rex W. Hagans and others, 1992, ED 354 631**

This program report describes five key dimensions for analyzing initiatives resulting in systemic change: infusiveness, pervasiveness, potency, coherence, and sustainability. It analyzes two strategies that exemplify effective systemic change—a school improvement and professional development bill in Oregon and an early childhood education and assistance program in Washington. $12.30. Northwest Regional Educational Laboratory, 101 Southwest Main Street, Suite 500, Portland, OR 97204; (503) 275-9500.

Statewide Restructuring of Education: A Handbook for Business, **Robert M. Palaich and others, 1990, ED 346 594**

This 24-page handbook (SI-90-8) offers practical information for businesspeople who want to support fundamental, collaborative education change. It discusses ineffective approaches and outlines effective strategies for business involvement to ensure that all children learn. $5.00, plus $2.50 handling. Education Commission of the States, 707 17th Street, Suite 2700, Denver, CO 80202-3427; (303) 299-3600.

Systemic Education Reform, **James Thompson, 1994**

This ERIC Digest (No. EDO-EA-94-5) introduces themes from systemic education reform and explores the implications for principals, superintendents, and school board members. $3.00. ERIC Clearinghouse on Educational Management, University of Oregon, 1787 Agate Street, Eugene, OR 97403; (800) 438-8841.

"Systemic Reform and Educational Opportunity," Jennifer A. O'Day and Marshall S. Smith, 1993, ED 359 626

This essay in *Designing Coherent Education Policy: Improving the System,* edited by Susan H. Fuhrman, advocates a systemic state approach in conjunction with greater professional responsibility on the local level to provide challenging content to all children. It explains how a coherent, coordinated approach can better serve less advantaged children than school-by-school restructuring. $32.95. Jossey-Bass Publishers, 350 Sansome Street, San Francisco, CA 94104; (415) 433-1767.

"Systemic School Reform," Marshall S. Smith and Jennifer A. O'Day, 1991

This ground-breaking essay in *The Politics of Curriculum and Testing,* edited by Susan Fuhrman and Betty Malen, outlines a design for a systemic state structure that supports school-site efforts to improve classroom instruction and learning. Key components of the design are unifying vision and goals, a coherent instructional guidance system, and a restructured governance system. $25.50. Falmer Press, 1900 Frost Road, Suite 101, Bristol, PA 19007-1598; (215) 785-5800. [A reprint of the chapter alone is available for $4.50 from CPRE, Carriage House at the Eagleton Institute of Politics, Rutgers University, 86 Clifton Avenue, New Brunswick, NJ 08901-1568; (908) 932-1331.]

Ten Years of State Education Reform, 1983-1993: Overview With Four Case Studies, **Diane Massell and Susan Fuhrman, 1994, ED 366 095**

This 171-page report examines the state of education reform and policymaking over the past 10 years, following publication of the landmark report, *A Nation at Risk,* in 1983. It examines the players involved, the capacity of the system to undertake reform, and the major instruments of reform, with case histories of activity in California, Florida, Georgia, and Minnesota. Recent trends in content-based reform, professional development, and assessment are explored. $15.00. CPRE, Carriage House at the Eagleton Institute of Politics, Rutgers University, 86 Clifton Avenue, New Brunswick, NJ 08901-1568; (908) 932-1331.

Transforming Education: Overcoming Barriers, Jane L. David and Paul D. Goren, 1993

This report examines efforts to restructure education and ways to counteract five barriers to school reform: lack of clear direction, weak incentives for change, regulatory and compliance mentality, limited learning opportunities for educators, and poor communication. $15.00, plus $4.50 shipping. National Governors' Association Publications, P.O. Box 421, Annapolis Junction, MD 20701; (301) 498-3738.

When School Restructuring Meets Systemic Curriculum Reform, Fred M. Newmann and William H. Clune, 1992, ED 348 711

This brief for policymakers explores two education improvement initiatives: school restructuring, which focuses on process in schools, and curriculum reform, which concentrates more directly on content. School restructuring is viewed as a means to build a teaching/learning environment that will support a high-quality curriculum. Free. Center on Organization and Restructuring of Schools, University of Wisconsin, 1025 West Johnson Street, Madison, WI 53706; (608) 263-7575.

CORWIN
PRESS

The Corwin Press logo—a raven striding across an open book—represents the happy union of courage and learning. We are a professional-level publisher of books and journals for K-12 educators, and we are committed to creating and providing resources that embody these qualities. Corwin's motto is "Success for All Learners."